Finally Free

Living Free and Loving Life

Kim Tabor

Word & Spirit Books
Tulsa, Oklahoma

Finally Free
Living Free and Loving Life
By Kim Tabor

ISBN: 978-1-936314-26-3

Cover design: Paige 1 Media

Interior design: Typography Creations

Edited by: Margie Knight
                KnightWriter@publish@gmail.com

Published and distributed by: Word & Spirit Books
                                   PO Box 701403
                                   Tulsa, OK 74170

Printed in Canada.

DEDICATION

*To the Living One who sees me each moment,
loves and knows me best, and
empowers me to live in freedom each day.*

ACKNOWLEDGEMENTS

I want to thank a few people that have been instrumental in the process of this book coming to life. First I want to thank Scott Blume for opening new doors for me in the publishing world. Keith Provance at Word & Spirit Books for being willing to have that first phone conversation with me and answering every single question I had, sometimes two and three times, thank you for your guidance. Margie Knight, your edits and valuable suggestions created a much stronger book. I can't thank you enough for using your talents on this project and for all of your time and patience.

Thank you, also, to Cheri and Jennifer. You were two of the first people to see my manuscript in its rawest form. You read every page and were gracious enough to make suggestions. Your positive responses gave me the courage to eventually get this book published. Also, to Tony and Misty, Larry and Jane, and to Roy and your beautiful Pam, who is now with the Lord; your continued prayerful support is overwhelming. Thank you all so much for believing in this ministry.

I want to especially thank Misty, Suzy, Sandra, Kathy, Missy, and Kristin for allowing me to share your stories. You are all beautiful women and I'm amazed by your courage and vulnerability. God continues to use each of you in a powerful way and it's a privilege to call you my friends.

Last, but not least, I want to thank my husband, Brian. I remember handing my manuscript to you. You were the very first to read it. I, also, remember seeing the tears in your eyes as you finished it. You're the only one who really knows the difficulty I had with choosing freedom. I had become comfortable with my bondage and freedom felt so foreign, but you kept challenging me to strive for all that God has for me. No one else has walked as closely with me on my freedom journey. You have seen me soar with success and driven to my knees with failure, but you've loved me just the same. Through both the beautiful and the difficult moments, you have been right by my side. You love me well and I'm eternally grateful that God sent you for me. You are truly my gift.

TABLE OF CONTENTS

My Story

"It is for freedom that Christ has set us free.
Stand firm, then, and do not let yourselves
be burdened again by a yoke of slavery."
GALATIANS 5:1

How did this happen? How did I get like this? Driving down the highway with tears streaming down my face, questions just kept running through my mind. These were tears of frustration and tears of release as I struggled to come to grips with some painful truths about myself for the very first time. I was so tired...tired of being afraid...tired of all the anxiety and worry...tired of feeling so badly about myself. My life looked much different at that point than I had ever intended, and when I gazed through the looking glass to examine the details, I didn't like what I saw. All of the fear, anxiety, and worry had stolen something very precious from me—something that was meant to be a gift.

As with each of us, God created me to fulfill His purposes by utilizing the gifts He placed within me. Singing is one of those gifts, but I had given it up years earlier because I couldn't deal with all the baggage that came along with it. I had allowed myself to be robbed of my God-given gifts. In the process, I let all of the insecurities and lies keep me from my destiny. But that morning in the car was my wake-up call.

A song started this emotional meltdown. It's funny when I think of the things God has used to speak to me during pivotal moments of my life, such as Scripture, people, events, and stories—anything He saw fit to use. How appropriate that He chose to use a song that day. As I was driving down the highway, the song *Free* by Steven Curtis Chapman came on the radio. At the end of the song, Steven sang the Scripture from John 8:36 over and over again: *"If the Son has set you free, you are free indeed. If the Son has set you free, you are free indeed."* As the tears flowed uncontrollably, I had the revelation that I wasn't free. God intersected my life at that moment and began to show me just how bound I was. I don't know why He chose that moment or that song. I just know everything began to change that day as I started to see things as they really were. I was living my life based on fear, anxiety, and worry. Even things that were supposed to be enjoyable became a source of fear for me.

From a very young age, I dreamed of making a difference for God and His Kingdom. I always knew I was going to serve Him in some way. As all children do, I began to figure out what some of my gifts were, and it became obvious music was going to be a part of whatever ministry God had planned for me. I dreamed of having a Christian concert ministry. I wanted to use music as a tool to give people hope and to introduce them to Christ, the One who had changed my life, but over time that dream became overshadowed by fear, doubt, and self-esteem issues.

Music has been important in my life for as long as I can remember. Actually, my mother tells me I started singing the same time I started talking. My parents at times tried to get me to sing in front of guests that came to our home, but I didn't like to be the center of attention. I would get terribly frightened and often became paralyzed by a childhood version of stage fright.

We moved a lot. My father worked for a large steel company when I was growing up, and the company transferred him every few years. Every new city meant a new school and new classmates to get to know. The moves were difficult for me because I didn't make friends easily. I learned early on that other children weren't drawn to the shy, awkward type like me. I soon discovered that if I could get up enough courage to do something to make myself stand out, the other children would like me. Singing was just the thing to do it.

It usually began in choir or music class. No matter what school I was in, the moment I opened my mouth to sing, typically so the music teacher could assign parts, I had instant friends. Sure, I was petrified, and I knew it didn't mean I had the greatest voice in the world. If I happened to be the best out of my class of 20 students, and it caused me to be accepted, then it was worth any case of nerves.

I didn't realize until much later how those early years had affected me. This overwhelming need to belong or to be liked continued to grow in my life. I just "knew" that for people to like me, love me, or care about me at all, depended on how well I could sing. I came to believe that people couldn't like me for who I was. If they liked me at all, it was only because I could sing.

This lie followed me into adulthood. With every song I sang, fear and anxiety set the hook deeper into my emotions. In my mind, my entire worth and value as a person was based solely on my singing. Soon, my body began to show signs of the fear I was trying to hold inside. While singing, my throat at times literally closed off in the middle of a song so that I physically couldn't sing. I was terrified. I lived with this extreme fear and anxiety for so many years that finally it was more than I could manage.

It was then that I made the very difficult decision to never sing again. I knew God had given me a gift, and His intent for that gift was for good—to see it bring glory and joy to Himself. In no small part, He also intended it to bring joy to me and those around me, but my gift became something I hated and was even afraid of. It was all because of a lie from the pit of hell itself—that no one could ever love me for "me" with or without the music.

Because of my struggle and different events in my life, I felt so horrible about myself that I couldn't fathom God using me for any kind of meaningful purpose. I believed that I had no value to God or anyone else, so I gave up singing, and more importantly I gave up on my dreams and God's purposes for my life.

Periodically, people still asked me to sing for events, and I always said no. That went on for years until one day a dear friend asked me to sing for a large event he was putting together. He refused to take no for an answer, so I told him I would think about it. I got in my car to drive home and began to concoct a plan in my mind for how to get out of singing for it. *It should be easy enough to come up with some kind of excuse,* I thought to myself. I decided I would deal with it later as I turned on the radio and started flipping through stations. That was when Steven Curtis Chapman's song caught my ear.

I believe there are defining moments in our lives— moments that not only change the trajectory of our lives but also begin to change our very hearts and souls. The first time I sang in my elementary school choir class was one of those moments for me. That was the moment I began to believe and become bound by a lie. When I found myself crying in my car, while listening to the Steven Curtis Chapman song as an adult many years later, was another defining moment. It was the moment God began to set me free.

In one of the chapters of Max Lucado's book titled, *When God Whispers Your Name,* he describes a sack of stones we all carry through life. Each stone represents a different painful thing or event. He describes how heavy our sacks become as we get older. This story really resonated with me, and I began to think about all the stones I carried in my own sack. Many things weighed me down, but fear and anxiety were by far the largest stones I carried.

That day in the car while listening to the song *Free,* God reached down and began to remove my stones—one at a time. He showed me that I was, in a sense, living a lie. I was a Christian and talked about being set free by Christ, but, in truth, I was still bound to the fear and lies. Thankfully, that's when God decided to intersect my life in this very unique way and impressed a few things on my heart, such as the difference between *talking about* a truth and *living out* a truth. It is one thing to say Christ has set me free, and it is another thing entirely to actually *live* a life of freedom *in Christ.* He revealed to me that my true worth and value as a person is wrapped up in Him and in what He did for me on the cross—not in anything I can do. He reminded me

His love goes higher, deeper, farther, and wider than I can ever imagine. I already knew all of these things because I had grown up in the church, but I began to realize there is a huge difference between *knowing* something in my mind and *knowing* it and *believing* it with all my heart. That day in my car was the first time I believed God loved me regardless of anything I could or would do, and that fact began to set me free. I ended up saying yes to my friend and sang at that event with a new-found freedom and assurance from God. That was the beginning of my freedom journey!

Notice that I said it was just the beginning. In my new journey into freedom, I've learned that freedom is a choice. I have the power to choose to live in freedom or to choose to live in bondage each day. The day after I sang at the event for my friend I noticed something else. After I sang, Satan left a big stone of fear sitting outside my door waiting for me. I had a choice to make. Do I pick up that familiar stone again or do I leave it there and walk past it? Even Christians can be bound by all sorts of things. I don't think I really believed that until the day I came face-to-face once again with that stone of fear. It was a very sobering moment. I had been a Christian for years but I was bound by wrong choices. It was my choice, and that's the bottom line. It begins and ends on my doorstep each day, and that's why I felt compelled to write this book. Freedom is ours if we choose it.

There is an enemy who hides at every corner ready to convince us that freedom isn't really attainable. He tries to tell us the way we are today is as good as we're ever going to get. He reminds us how comfortable we've become with our sack of stones and how dependent we are on them. He even tries to make us believe we actually enjoy the stones, and some of us buy into the lie. But the truth is most of us are tired of being weighed down by fear, anxiety, worry, bitterness, addiction...and the list goes on and on. The stones we've been lugging around are too heavy, and they were never meant for us to carry. In Matthew 11:28 Christ says, *"Come to me, all you who are weary and burdened, and I will give you rest."* Christ wants our burdens, but we must give them up willingly.

Do you truly want to live in freedom each day? Do you want to discover how to release the things that keep you from reaching your full potential? As you continue with me on this journey of discovering how to live each day in the freedom God intended for His children, I will share with you what God has been teaching me along the way. I hope these new-found truths will work for you as well. I believe you will also be blessed by testimonies from several other women, just like you and me, who have overcome and found freedom from a variety of difficult issues in their lives. God is no respecter of persons. What He does for one, He will do for all.

The key segments covered in the book are found in the acronym: FREE!

F—Focus (Seeing with Spiritual Eyes)

R—Restoration (Embracing Healing and Wholeness)

E—Enjoyment (Enjoying God and Life)

E—Empowerment (Becoming All God Intends Us to Be)

By the way, if you happen to be reading this book and you do not have a relationship with Jesus Christ, I hope you will stop right now and turn to Appendix A in the back of the book. There I explain what it means to have a relationship with the One who loves you more than life itself. It truly all begins there. None of the things in this book will be effective without a relationship with Him. The road to freedom begins with knowing and accepting Jesus Christ as your Lord and Savior. His Holy Spirit then will give you the wisdom, courage, and strength each day to choose freedom. There is no other way. I pray you will do that before you go any further in this book.

Let's continue on and see what God desires to teach each of us as heirs of His Kingdom. Thanks for walking with me, friends. The journey would be very lonely without you!

CHAPTER 1

FOCUS

SEEING WITH SPIRITUAL EYES

*"So we fix our eyes not on what is seen, but on
what is unseen. For what is seen is temporary,
but what is unseen is eternal."*

1 CORINTHIANS 4:18

Do you fix your eyes on what is seen or on what is unseen? If you are anything like me, I tend to get caught up in the hustle and bustle of everyday life and forget that I have more than one set of eyes. It happens to all of us. As each year passes, I've noticed I can't see as clearly with my physical eyes as I used to. I've always had 20/20 vision and have never worn glasses, but I'm already preparing myself for the reality of eventually wearing reading glasses. It's just one of the "perks" of getting older!

It's a good thing God gave me another set of eyes that won't dim with age to help guide me through life. I must admit I don't use them as often as I should, but with each passing day, I'm learning to look with my *spiritual* eyes and see beyond what my physical eyes can see. Another realm is out there that greatly impacts our lives but, to be quite candid, many Christians are completely unaware of it. Ephesians 6:12 says, "*For our struggle is not against flesh and blood, but against the rulers, against the authorities, against the powers of this dark world and against the spiritual forces of evil in the heavenly realms.*"

ANOTHER REALM IS OUT THERE THAT GREATLY IMPACTS OUR LIVES.

I am taking more seriously the spiritual battles that are around me each day, because there is an enemy who means us great harm, and we must be vigilantly on guard at all times. John 10:10 says, "*The thief comes only to steal and kill and destroy: I have come that they may have life and have it to the full.*" Satan himself is out to destroy us—not just hurt or wound us, but destroy us—and he begins at a very early age with many of us. He starts by planting little seeds of lies in our hearts. Even things or events that were meant for good can be turned and twisted by him to leave wounds in our hearts that, if untreated, will become gaping holes. Let me share with you one of these events from my own life.

A Seed Is Planted

I have always struggled with self-esteem issues. Growing up, I was very critical of myself, especially my appearance. When I was ten years old, my parents decided to enter me in a beauty pageant that was being held in our small town. They thought it would be something that I would enjoy. I was so excited about that day. The judges' scores were based on three different categories: appearance, talent, and the ability to answer a question on the spot.

I'm sure I sang a song for the talent portion of the competition, but honestly I don't recall what it was. I wore a beautiful, long yellow dress that my grandmother made for me. I must have done well during the first two rounds of appearance and talent because I advanced to the final round in which a judge would ask each of the five finalists a question. I watched each girl and listened as she answered what I thought were very easy questions, such as "What do you like to do?" and "What is your favorite television show?" I answered in my mind with ease each of their questions. I was the last one to be questioned. The judge stood in front of me, looked me in the eye and asked; "If you were the mayor of this city, what improvements would you make?" Complete silence filled the room.

What?! I thought to myself. *Where did that question come from? I'm 10! I've never even thought about the city before!* I stood in front of everyone—frozen in place. I didn't know what to say. Suddenly I felt extremely hot, and my face turned bright red as everyone stared at me. There is a reason the fear of public speaking is the number one fear of all fears! I couldn't think of one thing to say, so the judge repeated the question and looked at me again. Still nothing came out of my mouth. At that moment all I could think of was, *Say something! Say something!* It just kept going around and around in my mind, but I couldn't think of one thing to say...nothing...not a peep...not a sputter... nothing but dead silence.

I don't remember much after that. The judge must have given up at some point and ended the round. I was embarrassed and humiliated. I took fourth place. To make matters worse, I overheard one of the judges say to my dad, "If she just would have said something—anything—she would have won. She was in first place the whole time." I sobbed all the way home.

I didn't realize until years later how that one event affected the rest of my life. Satan had taken that opportunity to wound my heart with his taunts, "Not only are you not pretty, but you're stupid, and you can't speak in front of people either." The lies began, and I bought into them hook, line, and sinker. I never talked about that event again and just went on with life, but I very rarely spoke in public again. "Ask me to sing for something and I might consider it but don't *EVER* ask me to speak," became my mantra. The sad thing is I didn't really want to speak or sing in front of anyone. The thought of eyes staring at me just petrified me. What if something went wrong? What if I froze? What if people found out just how imperfect I was?

Do you see how Satan tries to take us out early in life? I couldn't see him with my physical eyes, but from a spiritual perspective, he was working overtime. I now make my living singing and speaking in front of people, but Satan started on me at the age of ten to try to make sure I would never become all God intended me to be. It wasn't until a few years after I was married that I allowed God to begin to heal that wound. He used my husband, Brian, to do it.

Terrified but Intrigued

Brian is a worship pastor, and during those years he was on staff at a church in Indianapolis. Our church had a great choir, and one day he called me from work and said, "Would you consider doing a devotional for our next choir rehearsal?" My immediate response was, *"What? Are you crazy?"* or something very similar to that! He then told me he felt very strongly that I was supposed to do this. I was terrified but also intrigued by the opportunity. Could I do this? Different thoughts and memories started racing through my mind. It's one thing to say a sentence or two to set up a song, which was the extent of my public speaking experience up until that point. But it's another to stand in front of a group for ten or fifteen minutes with something intelligent to say! Against my better judgment, I eventually told Brian I would do it.

I agonized over trying to prepare that first devotional. What would I say? Why would anyone even want to hear what I had to say? What if I didn't have enough to say? What if I sounded stupid? What if I said something that offended someone? The questions rolled around and around in my mind. I pulled out a few devotional books to gather some ideas. "You can do this, Kim," I kept telling myself. I spent days pouring through my Bible to find just the right passages. I practiced everything I would say word-for-word at least ten or twelve times before the night arrived. I even prepared little cheat sheets for myself. You would have thought I was getting ready to address the nation as the President of the United States with as much work as I put into this!

As I drove to the church that night, I began to get a sick feeling in my stomach. I knew it was anxiety, so I decided to stop and practice just one more time. There was a new cemetery right next door to our church. I wanted to be alone so I wouldn't be interrupted, and what better place to be alone than a cemetery! I pulled in, parked the car, and began to go over my notes. I wanted to literally practice it like I was going to say it in front of the choir, so I got out of the car and began to practice speaking all of my points complete with hand gestures. I must have been a sight! It's a good thing there was no one from the earthly realm around to see me—or so I thought. Right in the middle of my rehearsal, a car drove by; and the driver and passenger both gave me strange looks. This was back in the days before everyone had a cell phone, so I couldn't pretend I was just talking on my phone. As they stared at me, all I could think to do was smile and wave. They, however, didn't smile, and they didn't wave back. I'm sure they thought I was a madwoman talking to myself or a deceased relative! No doubt I was the topic of conversation in their car for a little while!

A Step of Faith

I finally decided I had practiced enough and it was time to just do it. I prayed and asked God to be with me and calm my nerves. I asked Him to help me speak intelligently so I could relay the message He wanted the choir to hear that night. I had done all I could do, so I drove next door to the church and went to choir practice. At the end of rehearsal, Brian called me up to speak. My hands shook as I stood in front of the fifty-or-so people in the room. I was petrified, but I took a deep breath and began to read. Suddenly, a funny thing started to happen. The more I read, the more I calmed down. I got through the reading and shared all of the points I had practiced over and over again. I even opened it up for questions! All in all, it seemed to go very well. No one fell asleep or threw anything at me or told me to sit down. (It's crazy the things that go through your mind when you're nervous!) I didn't freeze or draw a blank. No earth-shattering catastrophe occurred. Somehow

I survived the experience and actually enjoyed it. Who knew?! God knew.

Brian asked me to lead a devotional again the following week, and it eventually became a regular part of our choir rehearsals. That was the beginning of the healing of my wound and the facing of one of my fears. I took a step of faith. I took a chance on God and got out of my comfort zone. I prepared the best I could and then asked God to do the rest, and He did. I don't know why I ever doubted Him.

When I think about all of those years I wasted believing the lie that Satan had dangled in front of me, it makes me angry. I had focused only on what I thought I could see with my physical eyes and on the lies that I understood with my finite and deceived mind, instead of looking with my spiritual eyes and believing God.

Activating Our Spiritual Eyes

OUR SPIRITUAL EYES ARE, IN ESSENCE, GOD'S EYES.

How do we see with our spiritual eyes? Our spiritual eyes are, in essence, God's eyes. We must learn to see through His eyes and that can only be accomplished by the power of His Holy Spirit living within us. When I'm looking at myself, another person, or a particular situation in life with my physical eyes, I can easily become consumed with problem solving and worry.

That is when I need to consider Isaiah 55:8-9 which says, *"For my thoughts are not your thoughts, neither are your ways my ways,"* declares the Lord. *"As the heavens are higher than the earth, so are my ways higher than your ways and my thoughts than your thoughts."*

God's ways are different than our ways, and He looks at the world through a perfect set of lenses while our lenses are skewed by our personalities, our environment, or life circumstances whether positive or negative. Since we can't count on our own lenses, it's best to look through God's lenses, and the only way to do that is to allow His Holy Spirit within us to do the looking on our behalf. He sees things as they really are both in this life and in the spiritual realm. I can only see what is right in front of me and, most times, I don't even see that accurately. Through the power of His Holy Spirit, I focus on the One that brings true freedom and peace. I focus on His presence in my life and circumstances. I keep my eyes staid on Him and trust that He will give me the clarity I need to walk each day in the center of His will.

Do you truly believe there is more to this life than what can be seen with our physical eyes? Where are your eyes focused?

God Is Our Compass

Recently I was asked by our local ABC affiliate to record a jingle for their morning show, so I set up a time to go downtown to their studio to do the recording. I asked Brian to go with me. He agreed to go, but said we would have to drive separately because he would be coming straight from the church and would meet me at the studio. At this point, I should mention the fact that I'm a little "directionally challenged." North, South, East, and West don't mean much to me. Any directions I get are filled with lefts and rights. I truly am blessed that God allowed me to marry a man that's a human compass! If Brian has been to a city once, he can remember how to get around and where things are. He never gets lost. I, on the other hand, have major issues in this area.

When the day came for the recording, I left my house to drive to the studio to meet Brian. I don't drive downtown very often, so I got directions from the man at the studio and followed them explicitly. At least I thought I did. To make a long story short, I got lost. (I'm sure you saw that coming.) I missed my exit and ended up on the wrong highway! I won't bore you with all the embarrassing details. All you need to know is that I had no idea where I was. I got off the highway at the next exit, found a business building with a security gate, and pulled into the driveway. I asked the security officer if she knew how to get to the television station. She told me I was a long way from there, but she wasn't familiar enough with that part of town to give me directions. Thankfully, she allowed me to pull into the parking lot so I could call Brian and break the news to him. I reached him on his cell phone and tried to describe where I was. Much to my relief, he said he would come and find me. What a husband!

I got out of my car and stood by the street so I could flag him down when he drove by. Before long, I saw our black Suburban coming down the street. What a welcome sight to see that vehicle pulling into the lot! When he came to a stop, I told him the security guard had found a map if he needed it. He looked at me, shook his head back and forth and said, "I know exactly how to get there. I don't need a map. Follow me."

So that's exactly what I did. As I got into my car and followed him out of the parking lot, I didn't take my eyes off that Suburban. I didn't care which direction he was going or what route he was taking because I knew he would not lead me astray. History had shown me that the driver of the black Suburban knew where he was going, and he would never take me somewhere that would be harmful. I was so focused on the vehicle that he could have taken me down any crazy street he wanted, and I wouldn't have even noticed. I trusted him completely.

Who or what is your black Suburban? Where are your eyes focused? Hebrews 12:2 says, "*Let us fix our eyes on Jesus, the author and perfecter of our faith, who for the joy set before him endured the cross, scorning its shame, and sat down at the right hand of the throne of God.*"

I hope God is your black Suburban. History has proven that God can be trusted. He knows exactly where you need to go and how to get you there. Are you willing to go down streets you've never been on before? Are you willing to go a different route even if it means taking a step out of your comfort zone? As long as you keep your eyes on Him, it doesn't matter what street you're on or which turns you take; because you are confident that He knows where He is going. He would *never* lead you astray. Our God can be trusted, so we must focus our eyes on Him!

> HISTORY HAS PROVEN THAT GOD CAN BE TRUSTED.

The Eyes of Grace

Misty's story shows us how a fairytale journey can turn to destruction unless you have spiritual eyes to see beyond the pain of the present and focus on God's plan for redemption. I'll let her share how she found unexpected joy from what could have been a tragedy for her marriage and family.

❧❧❧

The beginning of my story with my husband is like a fairy tale—two young kids and love at first sight. We enjoyed our long distance relationship through high school, adjusted to life at the same college, then married soon after. We thought we knew how our story would read, and someday end, with both of us old and gray surrounded by the love of a big family and a lifetime of memories.

Six years into our journey, after a few job relocations and too many night shifts at work; we found ourselves "lost from each other." We were living two different lives. I have never felt so isolated, empty or alone. Many nights I cried and begged God to give my husband back to me. I remember telling Him, "No matter what…just bring him back."

The night before Thanksgiving that year, God began to answer my prayers—in a very painful way. Tony, my husband, came home from work with fear and dread in his eyes. He walked into the kitchen and just spilled out his confession, "I've had an affair, Misty, and she is going to have a baby." Everything froze, time stood still. This was not part of the story we had planned.

But God took what the enemy planned for evil and turned it into good. As I felt the next beat of my heart, I felt the Holy Spirit fill our kitchen; and then, I felt my heart fill with forgiveness. Over the next few hours, we cried and talked and cried some more. Tony asked if I wanted him to leave, but I asked him not to. I told him that although he had broken his vow to me, I would not break my vow to him.

That night in our kitchen, a new journey began in our lives. Over the next year we trudged through the deep waters of forgiveness and trust, rebuilding what Satan tried to destroy. As Tony recommitted himself to God and me, we began to grow closer than we had ever been. We committed to daily devotions and prayer time together, no matter how difficult. Through this dark and painful time in my life, God's voice came through loud and clear. Every day I heard from Him, proving "His mercies are new every morning." There was always a song on the radio, a Scripture from His Word or a message from a sermon that comforted me. One time God illuminated the story of Joseph in the book of Genesis. After all of the betrayal, lies, isolation, and fear he had been through, Joseph loved the Lord and trusted him. God blessed Joseph in tangible ways with wealth and authority, and then God gave Joseph another blessing—the blessing of forgetting your troubles and the pain attached to them (read the story in Genesis 41).

I can say to you now that God has caused me to forget my pain. Every time I see the wonderful blessing of the child that I did not carry in my womb, I remember the undeniable grace provided to me to carry him in my heart. Our family today is a testament to God's faithfulness, His never ending grace, and His power to heal. The child created in God's miraculous way is named Isaac, which means "he laughs," and boy, does he ever! He brings so much joy and laughter to our home. Only with God, do stories get written this way.

No one would choose to walk through the valleys. No one would choose to be empty, alone or broken. But when there is nothing left of us, we *see* more of God. We can experience qualities of Him that we never knew were there. We can *see* Him as our Restorer...our Healer...our Shelter...our Deliverer.

> WHEN THERE IS NOTHING LEFT OF US, WE SEE MORE OF GOD.

Freedom Fact: *"So we fix our eyes not on what is seen, but on what is unseen. For what is seen is temporary, but what is unseen is eternal,"* (2 Corinthians 4:18).

In your daily life, do you typically focus on what is seen or what is unseen?

What are the things that keep you from focusing on God at all times?

What three steps will you take on a daily basis for the next 21 days to shift your focus onto God? (It takes 21 days to change a habit.)

Freedom Prayer:

Dear Heavenly Father,

As I am journeying through this life, help me to be continuously aware of my focus. There is one who means me great harm, who uses fear and doubt to keep me consumed with my circumstances and people around me. Help me to focus my eyes on You alone. Thank You for guiding me, showing me where to turn and how to deal with different road-blocks along my path. I will follow wherever You lead, relying on Your lenses instead of my own skewed vision. Today I choose to focus on You, knowing You will never leave me nor forsake me!

Amen.

CHAPTER 2

RESTORATION

EMBRACING HEALING AND WHOLENESS

*"In my anguish I cried to the Lord,
and he answered by setting me free."*

Psalm 118:5

God wants to restore us. In terms of salvation, He has already provided restoration with the cross. Christ did everything it took to bring us back to Himself by dying on the cross and rising after three days, thereby conquering death. We can do nothing to save ourselves. We simply must choose to accept salvation as a free gift. What a Savior! I praise God for the free gift of salvation.

This chapter focuses on restoration as it relates to transformation. Webster defines restoration as the act of bringing back to an original condition. Although our complete restoration and perfection will not happen until we reach heaven, I believe God desires to begin the restoration process down here on earth by transforming us day by day.

The first time I realized I was supposed to be a transformed person; it was like a light bulb turned on in my head. The revelation that I should be more like Christ today than I was yesterday was life changing. I had accepted Christ many years before and knew I was going to heaven, but I never really thought about the fact that there was more after salvation. While we don't play any role in our own salvation except the role of gift receiver, I believe we play a vital role in our transformation process. God wants to partner with us while He is molding and shaping us. He won't force His way in or go where He's not wanted, so we must choose to partner with Him and allow Him to transform us.

> GOD WANTS TO PARTNER WITH US WHILE HE IS MOLDING AND SHAPING US.

Renewing the Mind

The mind is a powerful thing. Romans 12:2a says, *"Do not conform any longer to the pattern of this world, but be transformed by the renewing of your mind."* This has been my biggest battle. As a person that looks at the glass and sees it half empty instead of half full, I have never worked so hard to change anything about myself as I have worked to change my mindset. My mind is constantly battling with the rest of myself. I often joke about how I wish I could leave my head somewhere for a few hours just to give myself a break!

There truly is power in positive thinking, and great damage is done by negative thinking. I'm not talking about "name it and claim it" theology, and I'm not saying just because you think positively about something it's always going to work out the way you think it should. I'm talking about positive thinking as it relates to God. I believe negative thinking hinders the power of the Holy Spirit. In my own life, negative thoughts have been a result of low self-esteem and a lack of faith—not truly believing I'm worthy or that God has my best interest at heart in every circumstance. If we constantly entertain negative thoughts, always preparing for the worst instead of God's best, I believe we sell God short and quench His power that is within us.

Over the years I have developed certain recordings that play in my mind, many of which are negative. We all have such thoughts. They often begin as a result of lessons we learned from the world as we grew up or lies others taught us that we embraced. Many times the negative recordings are born out of our own insecurities because of seeds the enemy has planted in our mind. *You're not good enough. You'll never measure up. No one wants to hear what you have to say. You'll always be alone.* They go on and on. Before we even realize it, these recordings become our truth. We begin to believe them in every circumstance. Each day they start playing in our minds before we are even aware of them.

What are the recordings that play in your mind? I asked that question at a women's retreat one weekend, and you could have heard a pin drop. There was complete silence. Obviously, I had hit a nerve. I knew I was asking them to be vulnerable, and that it would be difficult. After a few moments, however, the floodgates opened. *She's more successful than you. You'll never be that successful. You're not a good mom. You're not a good wife. You can't do anything right. You're not attractive.* Those are just a few of the responses I got. Everyone has those recordings. They are extremely damaging and wreak havoc on us emotionally, mentally, and even physically. They affect our lives and the lives of those around us, as well as affecting our futures. It's time to erase them.

We must replace the negative thoughts that run through our minds with God's truth as it says in Philippians 4:8, *"Finally, brothers, whatever is true, whatever is noble, whatever is right, whatever is pure, whatever is lovely, whatever is admirable—if anything is excellent or praise-worthy—think about such things."* That is God's truth, and we should be thinking about true, noble, and pure things. Unfortunately many of us have become so comfortable with our negative thoughts that we can't fathom living without them, even though they're destroying us. We must find the courage to change how we think. There is no other way to be transformed. To replace the lies with the *truth,* we must go to God's Word.

I am still a work in progress, but I have made some huge strides in being transformed in recent years. Here are some things that have helped me along the way:

1. **I put signs up in strategic places around my house with Scripture written on them.** That way I can have a constant reminder of what I should be thinking about. Right now Galatians 6:9 is one of the Scriptures I have on the mirror in my bedroom. When the negative recordings start and I get discouraged wondering if God is really listening, I look to that verse which says, *"Let us not become weary in doing good, for at the proper time we will reap a harvest if we do not give up."*

   When I'm worried about a particular situation in my life and can't find any peace, and the recordings in my mind begin to encourage me to question whether God cares or whether He will intervene to work it out, I look to one of my favorite Scriptures, which is Philippians 4:4-7, *"Rejoice in the Lord always. I will say it again: Rejoice! Let your gentleness be evident to all. The Lord is near. Do not be anxious about anything, but in everything, by prayer and petition, with thanksgiving, present your requests to God. And the peace of God, which transcends all understanding, will guard your hearts and your minds in Christ Jesus."*

When those verses are put in strategic locations in my home, they are powerful reminders to me that God is in control and that I don't need to be anxious. I claim those verses as the truth, and I cling to them. To find more Scriptures dealing with specific issues, turn to Appendix B in the back of the book.

2. **I have also begun to pray and speak Scripture out loud.** This has been huge for me! Many of us have heard sermons preached about how sin begins to take root in a person. It begins as a thought, then it is verbalized, and then it becomes an action. I believe the same is true as it relates to a God-inspired transformation process. We begin by thinking it. We think the Scriptures and prayers in our minds; but when we begin to speak them out loud, things begin to change. It becomes embedded in our hearts at that point, and it becomes even more real to us when we declare it as *the* truth in our lives.

Psalm 35:28 says, *"My tongue will speak of your righteousness and of your praises all day long."* And Psalm 40:10a says, *"I do not hide your righteousness in my heart; I speak of your faithfulness and salvation."* And perhaps my favorite is Psalm 89:2, which states, *"I will declare that your love stands firm forever, that you established your faithfulness in heaven itself.*" The psalmist says he will declare it. That doesn't mean he will just think about it, but that he will state it emphatically.

I used to think the primary reason to speak about God's love and faithfulness was to encourage those around us and for the purposes of witnessing. Although that is definitely a great reason to do it, I now believe there is also another powerful purpose behind it. We speak out loud about God's love and faithfulness as a reminder to ourselves. We speak aloud His truths to remind ourselves that He is there and we are not alone—He does care and He is fully capable of transforming us.

Speaking the truth out loud through prayer and Scripture is a powerful step in renewing the mind, and it has helped me a great deal. Many times when the negative recordings have taken over, I've actually said out loud to myself, "Kim, you know that's not true. You are the apple of God's eye!" Zechariah 2:8b says, *"Whoever touches you touches the apple of his eye."* What a beautiful reminder of what we mean to God! Even whispering His name can help change our mind-sets. When I find myself caught in despair and unsure of what to do or say, I just whisper the name of Jesus; and it's like a healing balm to my mind and soul. There is great power in His name!

A friend from our previous church has taught me a great deal. Standing with her in our choir room one day, she was speaking to a woman who had questions about a particular situation in her own life. The woman didn't understand why things were happening the way they were, and she was really struggling. My friend looked at her and said, "I know you have a lot of questions. There are many things you don't know about this situation, so let's focus on what we *do* know."

Those words really touched me and made me think. Instead of focusing on what we don't know, let's focus our minds on what we *do* know. What do we know about God and how He works in situations? What do we know about the way He loves us as His children? I know what Scripture tells me. Isaiah 43:1b-3b says, *"Fear not, for I have redeemed you; I have called you by name; you are mine. When you pass through the waters, I will be with you; and when you pass through the rivers, they will not sweep over you. When you walk through the fire, you will not be burned; the flames will not set you ablaze. For I am the Lord your God, the Holy One of Israel, your Savior."*

THE TRUTHS FOUND IN SCRIPTURE NEED TO BECOME OUR NEW GOD-INSPIRED RECORDINGS!

God is with us. He has called us by name, and we are His. He knows us intimately. He will be with us as we pass through the waters and walk through the fire of this life. He will never abandon us! Those are some of the things we *do* know! Those are the things we need to focus on when the negative recordings threaten to play. The truths found in Scripture need to become our new God-inspired recordings!

2 Corinthians 10:4b-5 says, "*We demolish arguments and every pretension that sets itself up against the knowledge of God, and we take captive every thought to make it obedient to Christ.*" It's time to take our negative thoughts captive and turn them over to God!

Rebuilding the Heart

This world is painful. There's no getting away from it. You can't live on this earth and not have some wounds on your heart. It's impossible. Sometimes it seems as if all we do is hurt each other. Some of the deepest and most painful wounds can come from those we know best and love most. Those are the worst kind, and they take the longest to heal. Regardless of how many wounds we have, how deep they are, or how they got there; there comes a point in life when we have to deal with them. We have to say, "These are mine, I own them, and now it's time to start healing." God

GOD NEVER MEANT FOR HIS CHILDREN TO STAY IN A WOUNDED STATE.

never meant for His children to stay in a wounded state, and He certainly can't use us to our fullest potential if we walk around each day as a victim. We have got to let Him rebuild our hearts.

Many lives are shipwrecked by making bad choices. Suzy's testimony, as she shares it below, is just such an example of how God takes us through the refiner's fire during His process of restoration.

⚜

I look at life as a series of adventures. Each adventure has made me into the woman I've become. I was raised in a conservative Christian home and my parents were strict. My older sister pretty much followed the rules. I, on the other hand, challenged everything. I struggled with my spiritual life all through my teens and twenties. I was taught that salvation wasn't quite enough. I thought I had to be perfect and constantly felt like I didn't measure up and I got tired of trying. Life was more fun partying than trying to walk the Christian walk.

I was 18 years old when I met Eric, the cute captain of the football team. Our backgrounds were vastly different. We grew close anyway. It wasn't long until we were having sex.

The summer after my senior year I went to a global youth conference with my church. I knew I should break up with Eric and came home from the trip with a new commitment to God. Two weeks later I found out that I was two months pregnant. I had plans for college. Eric was going into his senior year of high school. I didn't want to tell my parents. So I went to a secular counseling center, and they convinced me that I needed to terminate the pregnancy. I remember sitting in a room full of other women after the procedure. We all passed around the Kleenex box and cried. It was the worst day of my life.

After I left for college, Eric, who my parents had forbidden me to see, would sneak up to visit. One too many visits and I was pregnant again. This time I knew I would marry him. I stood outside the door of the chapel on my Dad's arm the night of my wedding and wished I could call the whole thing off. So much felt "wrong," but I didn't want to be alone anymore either. So, we got married and I quit school. Our daughter was born while he was in his freshman year of college.

I soon discovered that Eric had a tendency toward lies, stealing, and abuse. Once, I was pushed down a flight of stairs in our apartment. Another time, he threw a coffee table at me. But, he never hit me, so I kept telling myself it was ok…I left him for a week.

During this time, we lived across the street from a Baptist youth pastor and his wife. She talked to me about God. I remember telling her, "If God is the same God I grew up with, no thank you." I was done with rules and regulations and never measuring up. Over several months, she loved me to the Lord. My life has never been the same.

After Eric graduated from college, I thought perhaps another child would "settle" him down. Our son was born, but the abuse continued to escalate. We separated twice over the next three years. A counselor encouraged me to go back to college in order to plan for my future. In the spring of my first year back in school, we had another crisis; and I took the kids and went to my parents so I could get through finals. Within two days, Eric had a woman living in our home. It was then that I filed for divorce.

A few years later, I met a wonderful man named John. After six years of marriage, I found myself in the midst of a fight of another kind. I was diagnosed with rectal cancer, but the doctor thought he had "gotten" it all. Shortly thereafter, I found out that the cancer had metastasized to both of my lungs. It was during the first surgery that God revealed himself to me in a new way. One evening while in the ICU, I had a panic attack. My mom was in the room, and she began to sing "Jesus loves me." I felt myself being rocked in His arms. I was able to relax and the panic attack went away. I knew that no matter what I went through in this life, He would always be there.

Through all of my "adventures" in life, I have learned that only through the fire can I be made like gold. The fire hasn't been pleasant and many times it was very painful, but I know I am stronger because I made it through. I have two beautiful children and an incredible husband who cherishes all three of us. I have finally found a way to accept God's forgiveness and to heal from the abortion I had all those years ago. Today, I am also cancer free.

God is amazing and I am humbled every time I think about how much He loves me. I can't wait until that day that I get to see Him face to face, wink and grin and say, "Thanks, Daddy!"

Many people have had devastating things happen to them, and it takes a long time and a lot of counseling to deal with those issues. I believe in Christian counseling, and I know many that have been changed and are on a healthier path today because of it. While there is a place for Christian counseling, I want to focus right now on God's counseling and the very important role He plays in our healing. He is the Wonderful Counselor. In John 14:26 Christ says, *"But the Counselor, the Holy Spirit, whom the Father will send in my name, will teach you all things and will remind you of everything I have said to you."* God will counsel us through His Holy Spirit.

I've had a number of painful things happen to me that created deep wounds in my heart. Some wounds were immediately apparent, and the results were devastating. Others, however, grew over time and stayed hidden for many years. They actually became a part of the fabric of my being, and it's taken a long time to heal those wounds and change old habits that were formed because of them.

How do we begin to heal? How does God counsel us? One of the things I did was to journal about all of the painful things I could remember happening to me in my past—things that I felt really affected me. The process of writing those events down was very therapeutic for me and helped me to get them outside of myself. Experiences and events can get trapped inside of us, and we must get them out in order to look at them more objectively.

Around the same time I began journaling, I read a book by John Eldredge called, *Waking the Dead*. In this book he takes the journaling process a step further. He talks about going through the painful events in our lives and inviting God there. He writes, "We need time in the presence of God...When we are in the presence of God, removed from distractions, we are able to hear him more clearly, and a secure environment has been established for the young and broken places in our hearts to surface...Then we invite Christ in. We ask Jesus to come into the emotion, the memory, this broken place within us. We give him permission; we give him access."[1]

I began to invite God into my broken places. I pictured Him there with me, and I asked Him to heal me. It truly has been an amazing process. I have pictured Him crying with me when I've cried and getting angry along with me when I've been angry. I asked Him to bring healing and to help me let go. This exercise reminded me just how real He is in every moment of my life—that He is intimately aware of all of the details no matter how heart wrenching. He cares deeply about my wounds, and He desires to bring me back to a place of wholeness.

I can only be whole when I've allowed my wounds to be healed. And yes, I have to allow it to occur. I have to choose to let those events go and to realize that although they will forever be a part of my past, I can no longer let them control me and my future. I must come to a place of forgiveness and that includes forgiving others as well as myself. Others have wounded my heart time and time again, but there has also been plenty of self-inflicted wounding through the years. Part of the healing process is asking for and learning to accept God's forgiveness for my own devastating choices and in turn forgiving myself and others as He has forgiven me.

God has slowly begun to repair my heart. He has illuminated different Scriptures to me that I have claimed during my healing process. He has whispered His love to me in so many different ways and I know He'll do the same for you. He has a deep desire to restore His children.

⁂

Freedom Fact: Isaiah 61:1 *"...He has sent me to bind up the brokenhearted, to proclaim freedom for the captives and release from darkness for the prisoners."*

What are some Scripture verses that encourage you when times get tough? Write a few of them down and place them in strategic places in your home as a reminder of God's promises.

If you still have wounds on your heart that haven't healed yet, I challenge you to begin journaling and asking God to join you in your most painful places to begin the healing process.

Freedom Prayer:

Dear Heavenly Father,

I know You desire healing and wholeness for me. Let today be the first day of my restoration process. I will hold fast to the eternal truths that I find in Your Word to begin to change the age-old negative recordings that play in my mind. I will no longer think damaging thoughts about myself or others. You created us and love us. I choose to think about things that are true, noble, right, pure, lovely, admirable, excellent, and praiseworthy. I give You control of my mind and ask that You help me to make a conscious choice each day to develop new thought habits— Ones that will glorify and please You.

Bind up the wounds of my heart whether they were self-inflicted or as a result of others. I invite You to do a miraculous healing that only You can do in the most secret places of my heart and mind. I choose a path of healing and forgiveness today. Forgive me for poor, rebellious choices that I have made in the past. (Confess any specific sins that come to your mind.) I will choose a better path from this day forward. Thank You for forgiving me and washing me clean. Just as You have forgiven me, I choose now to forgive myself and others that have wounded me. Psalm 103:12 says, *"as far as the east is from the west he has removed our transgressions from us."* Since you don't keep any record of my sins, I choose to forgive others and release them to You. I will NO LONGER live as a victim. I choose to live a victorious life of freedom through You!

Amen.

CHAPTER 3

Enjoyment

ENJOYING GOD AND LIFE

"Be joyful always; pray continually;
give thanks in all circumstances,
for this is God's will for you in Christ Jesus."
I THESSALONIANS 5:16-18

How long has it been since you had a really good belly laugh? Children, for the most part, have a pretty clear understanding of how to have fun and enjoy the days God has given them. So why is it that most adults have a harder time enjoying life than when they were kids? We grow up, get jobs, pay bills, get married, and have kids; as well as try to live for God and make time for Him. We strive to get ahead in life and make more money to buy bigger houses and nicer cars, as we try to be a better parent, spouse, and friend to all. Our lists are incredibly long and overwhelming. Before we know it, we've become dissatisfied and disappointed with everything around us. We realize it's been months since we've really connected with our spouse, and years since we've enjoyed our lives—not to mention the Creator of our lives, if that is even possible. We begin to wonder how we got to this place. Where did our joy go?

Acts of Enjoyment

The act of enjoyment is important because it helps us become more grateful, which in turn keeps us from complaining and criticizing constantly. We take ourselves far too seriously. We should learn to lighten up and laugh and love more.

My husband is an expert on the subject of enjoyment. We have a standing joke between us that it's a good thing God put us together, because without him, I would have no idea how to have any fun. I have a more difficult time enjoying life, but Brian has helped to loosen me up a bit. He looks for ways to have fun, and he *loves* a good party. It touches me deeply that he celebrates me with surprise birthday parties and in other special ways, but I have to tell you that he also loves to celebrate and enjoy God. He takes every opportunity to stop and honor the things God has accomplished in and for us; and we have seen the fruit of this in our lives. Many times we've prayed for something specific and have seen God work miracles. I must admit I often look at those occasions and check them off my "to do list" and move on to the next thing. Brian doesn't do that. He stops and enjoys the moment, giving thanks to God.

Sometimes it's a little easier to think about celebrating something once it has been accomplished. That's why we have going-away parties, retirement, and graduation parties. It makes sense to enjoy those moments before moving on to the next chapter of life. As Brian has demonstrated the importance of celebrating the moment, I've also found that there has to be enjoyment *during* the process as well. The journey is just as important as the destination. The process is just as important as the product. Many of us struggle to enjoy the journey. We're so focused on the destination that we miss out on all God has for us as we travel together in our day-to-day lives.

> THE JOURNEY IS JUST AS IMPORTANT AS THE DESTINATION.

Enjoying God

I don't spend enough time enjoying God. To be quite candid, until recent years I never thought about enjoying Him. For some reason, the whole concept was foreign to me. When we first become Christians, many of us have a constant struggle to stay intimate with God. Actually that struggle continues to some degree for most of our lives. It can be difficult to remember that He *is* here with us no matter what we're experiencing. Often we tend to picture Him being very far away, someone who not only can't be grasped, but who is also not accessible. That's just not true. Our minds may not be able to grasp all that He is. I may not be able to see Him with my physical eyes or touch Him, but He *is* here. Proof of His presence is all around us.

PROOF OF HIS PRESENCE IS ALL AROUND US.

Hebrews 11:1 tells us, *"Now faith is being sure of what we hope for and certain of what we do not see."* God is with us and He knows us better than we know ourselves. Psalm 139:13 says, *"For you created my inmost being; you knit me together in my mother's womb."* He made us, *knows* us intimately, and He wants us to *know* Him the same way. He wants us to love and enjoy Him.

I've discovered there is only one way to learn to enjoy God—which for me is a learning process—and that is to spend time with Him. There is no other way to do it. Sometimes spending time with Him is the last thing we seek to do. It's our last resort when it should be the thing we most look forward to doing. I need to spend time talking with Him, studying His Word, and listening for His voice in order to keep my life on track. The more we do those things, the more we will come to know and enjoy Him in a more meaningful way.

Relationships Have History

There is a difference in how I feel about someone I've just met and someone I've known for many years. When I first meet people, it takes me time to figure them out, to discover what they like or don't like and what makes them laugh. After a period of spending time with a person, however, there is a deepening in the relationship. We begin to have a history together. We can know what the other is thinking with just a look, and we can laugh easily together either in the moment or by recounting funny memories. The time together becomes natural and easy. It's enjoyable, not forced. The more we're together the more we begin to enjoy each other's company, and you can tell a lot about a person by the company they keep. It's an interesting phenomenon, but we truly do become a lot like the ones with whom we spend the most time.

I was blessed to have a wonderful college roommate. I consider her one of my closest friends to this day. We lived together during most of college and then for a few years after we graduated. We laughed every time someone mistook us for sisters. We really don't look anything alike! I'm blonde with blue eyes while she's brunette with brown eyes. I could give you a whole list of areas where we are completely different when it comes to our appearance, but after more than six years together, I guess we started to resemble each other in different ways; such as in our mannerisms, personalities, taste in clothing, and even our speech! People often told us how much alike we were, but, quite honestly, neither one of us realized it.

You really get to know someone when you live together. You can't hide much, so you experience all aspects of that person; and the next thing you know, you begin to rub off on each other. God wants us to know Him that well and He wants to do more than just rub off on us. He wants to penetrate our very beings and change us to be more like Him. He wants us to enjoy spending time with Him—to know Him so intimately that we know what makes Him laugh, what's important to Him, and how He loves. He wants us to be able to recognize His still small voice in the midst of the screams of life. I want to come into and enjoy His presence by knowing Him in that manner; don't you?

Overflowing Praise

When I began to think about all the different people I enjoy spending time with, I realized how the praise just begins to flow from my lips about them. "You are so funny! You can really make me laugh and I love that," I said to a friend recently.

A few months ago, I was at a restaurant and enjoyed one of the best meals I've ever had. I *love* food! The chef was walking around conversing with the guests. He came to our table and I began going on and on about the food saying, "You're an incredible chef! This is one of the best meals I've ever had!" He beamed as the words of praise came out of my mouth. I didn't even know him, but the praise was easy. How much more easily I should praise God. I want the praise to just flow from my lips because of all He's done for me and who He is in my life. I want to feel delight and gladness while I'm praising Him and that means I *must* learn to enjoy Him. If I am spending time with Him and am learning to legitimately enjoy Him, then the praise should just come flowing out from my lips and heart. He deserves at least that much from me!

Enjoying Life

I love women's retreats. There is nothing like spending the weekend with a group of ladies laughing and crying together. When you get them away from their husbands, kids, jobs, and household responsibilities, they are ready to cut loose! A few months ago while speaking at a retreat, I decided to try an experiment with the ladies in attendance. I wanted to see how much they could enjoy themselves— really let their hair down and just have fun! Music is such a powerful tool, and I decided to play some secular music clips for the ladies to see what memories would come to mind and how they would respond. When I played the first clip, immediately a smile came across almost every face. You could see the wheels begin to turn in their minds. They were taken back to a day when they felt freer, had fewer responsibilities, and enjoyed life unhindered. The hands shot up, and people told stories of their lives that went along with each song. The whole demeanor of the room changed. Women were laughing and reminiscing. A whole new realm of freedom and lightheartedness was displayed.

When the last clip was played, nothing could have prepared us for what was about to happen. All of a sudden, a woman at the front of the room jumped up and started dancing. The next thing we knew a conga line formed, and they started dancing around the room laughing and singing! What a sight! I will never forget seeing such joy and abandonment. Those women were enjoying themselves to the fullest, and I believe the Lord was pleased to see His children having fun. There were no scowls and there was no judgment—just good, clean fun!

Our homes and our churches should be filled with that kind of joy and excitement. We need to replace our worry with more enjoyment. I know life is hard and serious and at times very painful, but we can't forget that even in the midst of tough situations we have so much for which to be grateful. God has allowed us to wake up today, and He wants to laugh with us on this journey. He loves us and we are His children. It's time to rejoice in that and allow ourselves to enjoy this life He's given us! His Word confirms it in John 15:11-12, which says, *"I have told you this so that my joy may be in you and that your joy may be complete. My command is this: Love each other as I have loved you."*

Even if it's just a few minutes each day, it's good to "stop and smell the roses" by giving ourselves permission to do things that might be looked at by some as frivolous. It's okay to take a soothing bath, get a massage, have a manicure, read a few pages from a book, close our eyes for a few moments to clear our minds, or go to lunch with a friend. It's important to feed our souls in the midst of our chaotic lives. We won't have much to offer our friends, family, or God if we don't take care of ourselves and learn to enjoy our days.

God Is Faithful!

Time is fleeting. We never know when our lives might be interrupted by a tragic accident or even death. Our dear friend, Sandra, was on her way to work on the morning of October 18, 2008, and felt compelled to thank God for good health. She was active and very healthy as she was soon approaching her 60th birthday. She felt blessed and offered a quick prayer of thanksgiving. Sandra is one of those people that exude joy abounding and running over.

In a conversation with her son that day at the church office complex where she serves as the women's ministry director, she ended their discussion by saying, "God is faithful!" As she started down the stairs to go to the parking lot to meet her husband, just five steps from the bottom, she tumbled to the floor and hit her head so hard she went unconscious and began to bleed from her ears, nose, and mouth. Her heart stopped and the paramedics had to resuscitate her before rushing her to the hospital.

In ICU the doctors put her on a ventilator and inserted a brain cavity pressure sensor to monitor her brain activity. She began to have seizures and lapsed into a coma. The trauma to her body was so severe, only the machines were keeping her alive. After four days, the doctors told her family that she had sustained the worst possible brain injury. The fall had caused her brain stem to literally separate from her brain, a condition that is irreversible. They said if she was removed from the machines, she might live 24-36 hours; and if she somehow survived, she would be in a vegetative state unable to walk, talk, or have any memory of family or friends. The doctors advised her family to start planning her funeral because they wanted to wean her off the machines.

Her family and those in her church family refused to accept this dire report. The Sunday night service was dedicated to prayer for Sandra's healing and recovery. The next day the doctors began weaning her off the machines. A battery of tests was run, and the doctor was amazed at what he saw. Some brain damage was evident, but he couldn't find any significant damage to her brain stem. During the night, God had knitted her brain stem back onto her brain.

From that day forward, dramatic improvements took place. After four weeks in a coma, she began to respond to verbal commands to open her eyes and wiggle her fingers and toes. Each day she was a little more awake. The doctors described her progress as astonishing. Her improvement continued with a few setbacks along the way, but the Lord overcame every obstacle as she was released from the hospital and continued therapy in a rehabilitation facility.

On December 23rd Sandra left the rehabilitation facility for good, healed by the hand of a Mighty God! Here is how Sandra described her journey:

"I was able to celebrate my Savior's birth at home with my husband, children, and grandchildren. I was even able to attend church on Christmas Eve where my family walked me out on the platform, and I loudly proclaimed the verse that I had come to live by over the past few months from Psalms 118:17: *I shall not die, but live and declare the works of the Lord.*

"The doctors gave me no hope, but by the hope and promise I have in Jesus, I came home whole! Except for the fall itself and the weeks I was in a coma, my memory is intact. I still have the same personality and sense of humor. I am back both mentally and physically. I can say without a shadow of a doubt, my God *is* faithful!"

Sandra continues to enjoy life to its fullest and testify of God's faithfulness to all who will listen.

Mine for the Gold

For those who are married, I want to say a quick word about enjoying our spouses because I believe it goes hand in hand with enjoying our lives. Marriages are under attack like never before, and many husbands and wives are living together as nothing more than roommates in their own homes. Marriage can be difficult and requires deliberate effort by both spouses to be successful. God's intention is for us to enjoy each other. The best way to do this is to mine for the gold in our spouses, rather than the deficiencies.

Brian and I are such different people, and it's still amazing to me that God can knit together two totally different lives in the form of marriage. When I first started dating Brian, I was absolutely infatuated with him. I couldn't find one thing wrong with him or think of anything he needed to improve. I know that sounds crazy, but for the first six months we dated I thought he was perfect! Now, after many years of marriage, we each could write a book detailing each other's deficiencies. My how things change with the passing of time!

I'm sad to say there have been occasions when the deficiencies are the only things I focused on instead of all of his good characteristics. I've learned that most people know what their deficiencies are. So, why do I feel the need to point them out? I try hard not to do that any longer. The key to compatibility and peace is to focus more on the positive and less on the negative as it relates to our spouses. I've seen women speak in a degrading way to their husbands in public and then seen the dejected looks on the husbands' faces. We will discover *many* good things if we truthfully look for them. An encouraging word will bring the gold to surface more often than the dirt. I don't know what I would do without my husband. He is still the love of my life and my gift from God, so I make every effort to treat him that way!

> AN ENCOURAGING WORD WILL BRING THE GOLD TO SURFACE MORE OFTEN THAN THE DIRT.

Rock My World

Kathy and her husband have been dear friends for years. Kathy believed being a naval officer's wife and mom of two great kids was the greatest thing she could do, but there was a tug on her heart to do something more. She still wanted to be totally flexible to car pool and be at home when her kids came home each day, so she explored starting an in-home sales business. Fear and faith had a field day, struggling inside her heart and mind, as she thought of all the excuses in the book not to proceed. Finally, faith won out and she gave herself permission to step out and see what God would do. She got involved and loved the people she worked with in building the business.

She even found the courage to keep going after they moved to a new city.

When Kathy's children left for college, her business helped her overcome the "empty nest syndrome." She was able to enjoy her business even more as she focused on others and their needs and was reminded that God was in control. The business has blessed the family in so many ways. Kathy's husband recently shared this story with us.

Kathy frequently flies out of state for national meetings, and one year he went with her because Kathy, along with some other directors, was going to be acknowledged for her work with the company. At one of the sessions, all of the husbands were asked to introduce their director wives who were being recognized, so our friend began to think of a special way to introduce his precious wife. One by one each husband took a moment to say some nice things about their wives in front of the large crowd assembled. Then it was our friend's turn. He got up, pointed to Kathy, and yelled, "This is my wife and she ROCKS MY WORLD!" The whole place erupted and she stood there with a huge smile on her face! What that must have meant to her!

Our spouses need that sort of acclamation. Can you imagine what it would do to your husband if you told him he ROCKS YOUR WORLD? I tried it with mine in an e-mail one day, and his reply said, "I feel like I can conquer the world now!" Make it a point to enjoy and appreciate your spouse each and every day. Be creative and think of ways to "rock his world"!

Women Need Women

I love talking about enjoyment! Can you tell? God and my husband are teaching me how to enjoy my life, and that is a huge part of the journey to freedom! Enjoying life includes enjoying the people that are in our lives like our spouses and others that are around us—especially our sisters in Christ. Women need each other. Female relationships can be hard at times, but we shouldn't let that keep us from experiencing all God has for us within those relationships. My husband frequently lets me know how glad he is God made him a man and not a woman because women are too complicated. We tend to judge each other and compare ourselves to one another and spend far too much time tearing each other down instead of lifting each other up! God didn't create us to be an island unto ourselves. He created us to need each other. It is important for us to know others and to be known by others. Finding women we can trust and entering into a healthy friendship with them helps to sustain us through the good and the tough times.

> GOD DIDN'T CREATE US TO BE AN ISLAND UNTO OURSELVES.

In addition to finding women we can trust, we must be the kind of women that can *be* trusted. When someone tells us something in confidence, it is important to keep our lips shut and maintain that confidence. To have a friend, we must be a friend—the kind of friend we desire for ourselves. Learning how to forgive quickly and how to hang in there with our friends will allow us to move on past the hurts. We are going to hurt each other at times. It just happens. Henry Ward Beecher, a pastor and abolitionist, once said, "Keep a fair-sized cemetery in your backyard, in which to bury the faults of your friends." No one is perfect—not even our friends. We need to concentrate more on being the best women we can be and less on the faults and failures of those around us. We should mine for the gold in other women just as we do with our spouses.

The Beauty of a Cracked Pot

I recently read a story from India in a book by Brennan Manning titled, *Ruthless Trust*. The story is called The Cracked Pot and the author of the story is unknown.

A water-bearer in India had two large pots. Each hung on opposite ends of a pole that he carried across his neck. One of the pots had a crack in it, while the other was perfect. The latter always delivered a full portion of water at the end of the long walk from the stream to the master's house. The cracked pot arrived only half-full. Every day for a full two years, the water-bearer delivered only one and a half pots of water.

The perfect pot was proud of its accomplishments, because it fulfilled magnificently the purpose for which it had been made. But the poor cracked pot was ashamed of its imperfection, miserable that it was able to accomplish only half of what it had been made to do.

After the second year of what it perceived to be a bitter failure, the unhappy pot spoke to the water-bearer one day by the stream. "I am ashamed of myself, and I want to apologize to you," the pot said.

"Why?" asked the bearer. "What are you ashamed of?"

"I have been able for these past two years to deliver only half my load, because this crack in my side causes water to leak out all the way back to your master's house. Because of my flaws, you have to do all this work, and you don't get full value from your efforts," the pot said.

The water-bearer felt sorry for the old cracked pot, and in his compassion, he said, "As we return to the master's house, I want you to notice the beautiful flowers along the path." Indeed, as they went up the hill, the cracked pot took notice of the beautiful wildflowers on the side of the path, bright in the sun's glow, and the sight cheered it up a bit.

But at the end of the trail, it still felt bad that it had leaked out half its load, and so again it apologized to the bearer for its failure.

The bearer said to the pot, "Did you notice that there were flowers only on your side of the path, not on the other pot's side? That is because I have always known about your flaw, and I have taken advantage of it. I planted flower seeds on your side of the path, and every day, as we have walked back from the stream, you have watered them. For two years I have been able to pick these beautiful flowers to decorate my master's table. Without you being just the way you are, he would not have had this beauty to grace his house."[1]

Brennan Manning responds to this story by saying, "The pot had assumed that the sole purpose of its existence was to haul water from the stream to the house. Enfolded within its narrow self-determination, the flawed pot had not suspected God's grand purpose for it—to give life to the dormant flower seeds along the path. The cracked pot was sad because it compared itself to the perfect pot. Without the comparison, it would have been happy, content in the knowledge that it was exactly the way it was supposed to be."[2]

COMPARING OURSELVES TO ONE ANOTHER CAN BE DANGEROUS.

Comparing ourselves to one another can be dangerous. There are moments when we must put ourselves up against someone who is stronger, faster or better than we are so that we can stretch and grow, but I'm not talking about those situations. I'm referring to a mindset that focuses on comparisons. *She is prettier than me. She is thinner than me. She is more talented than me.* Judging is not our role, and it's a waste of time. We're taught to make comparisons in our culture today and we must fight against that!

Romans 12:4-6b says, *"Just as each of us has one body with many members, and these members do not all have the same function, so in Christ we who are many form one body, and each member belongs to all the others. We have different gifts according to the grace given us."* We all are very important members of the same body. It is time to stop comparing ourselves to one another and remember that my gifts are for your edification and your gifts are for mine. Our gifts are for each other so there should be no envy, jealousy, or comparison. I know that is easier said than done. I fall victim to this at times as well, but we've got to guard against it.

Noted author, Joyce Meyer once said, "God will help you be all you can be—all you were originally designed to be. But He will never permit you to be successful at becoming someone else." God has an individual plan for us and for those around us. We are meant to lift each other up and enjoy those who are walking beside us on this journey called life!

Freedom Fact: *"Delight yourself in the Lord and He will give you the desires of your heart,"* (Psalm 37:4).

Take some time right now to spend with God. Pour your heart out to Him. Listen for His still small voice. Seek His face—not just His hand. Enjoy your time with Him.

Spend time this week enjoying those around you, whether it's spending one-on-one time with your spouse telling him how he rocks your world, or spending time with a girlfriend encouraging her and lifting her up!

Freedom Prayer:

Dear Heavenly Father,

Thank You for this day! I want to live each moment of it enjoying Your presence in the details of my journey. I celebrate You today for who You are, for all You have done in my life, and all that You will continue to do. You are worthy to be praised, so my lips will praise You, my Lord and my God!

I thank You for the relationships You have placed in my life. I am forever grateful for my precious family! Give me an opportunity today to pour joy into their lives. I thank You for my friends. So many need encouragement, and I am up to the task! Help me to look at each of my sisters as allies and not adversaries, remembering that I need her just as much as she needs me. I thank You that You created us for relationship with You and others! Help me to strive for healthy relationships where there is open and honest communication, love, trust, and vulnerability. I choose to BE the kind of friend I desire to have.

I will enjoy the days You have given me while basking in Your presence and allowing Your love to overflow from my life into the lives of those that cross my path! Thank you, Father, for Your love and for giving me a reason to enjoy life!

Amen.

CHAPTER 4

Empowerment

BECOMING ALL GOD INTENDS US TO BE

*"I can do everything through Him
who gives me strength."*

PHILIPPIANS 4:13

Do you want to make a difference in the lives of your family, those you come into contact with in the world around you and in God's Kingdom? I'm so thankful that He doesn't just see who I am today, but He sees all I *can* be through Him. He gives us all the power we will ever need through His Holy Spirit. God can't fully use us when we are bound or weighed down by the stones of life. As we release our stones to Him, He lightens our loads so we can display His splendor and glory. Saint Irenaeus once said, "The

THE GLORY
OF GOD IS
MAN FULLY
ALIVE.

Glory of God is man fully alive." I believe the only way to be fully alive is to be truly set free.

I want to be a *difference maker* in this world for God and His Kingdom. My heart's desire is to love like He loves, to bring His hope into hopeless situations, and to show compassion and mercy like He has shown to me. I wrote this book so you can join me on this quest. People all around us are dying spiritually and physically each day with no hope. They need someone to be Jesus' hands and feet in their lives, to bring them the hope only He can deliver. As His children, we can do *all* things through Him who strengthens us. I want to live the fullest life God has for me, and I want to be a positive example for the generations that follow. We can do this as we claim Psalm 71:18 for ourselves, *"Even when I am old and gray, do not forsake me, O God, till I declare your power to the next generation, your might to all who are to come."* Living in freedom empowers us to make a lasting difference in the lives of those around us!

A Daughter of the King

Driving to church one Sunday morning by myself, I exited the highway and stopped at the light at the end of the off-ramp. There were a few cars in front of me at the light. As I sat there, I could see a woman standing at the corner of the ramp, asking people for money. Homeless people frequent this location often holding signs or moving from vehicle to vehicle asking for money, so that didn't surprise me, but I had never seen this particular woman before. Something about her caught my attention and I felt very drawn to her. As I watched her, I saw the window of one of the vehicles in front of me go down. As a hand from inside the car threw change out at the woman, it went flying and landed in the dirt by the side

> LIVING IN FREEDOM EMPOWERS US TO MAKE A LASTING DIFFERENCE IN THE LIVES OF THOSE AROUND US!

of the ramp. The woman quickly dropped on her hands and knees and started to scour the dirt, looking for every coin she could find. I sat there and watched as this woman, created in the image of God, scrounged through the dirt like a wild animal trying to collect scraps of food someone had just thrown out. I thought as I watched this scene: *She is the daughter of the King and she doesn't even know it. She has never claimed her inheritance, that precious gift that God freely offers all of us. How did she get like this? And what possessed someone to throw money at her like she was less than human?*

I sat in my car and started to cry. I knew I had to talk to her. I drove to the church, which was only a short distance away, and found a male friend of ours who was available and asked him to go back to the ramp with me.

Although I wanted to talk with her, I also knew it was wise to take some precautions, because I really didn't know what I was getting myself into. The two of us drove back down the highway a few minutes later, and I got out of the car. I approached the woman, put out my hand, and introduced myself. She looked at me, shook my hand, and told me her name was Lorraine. I was dressed for church, and she took one look at my clothes and said, "You've got to get out of here. You'll mess up my money. No one will give anything to me with you standing here."

We then began a dialogue that I will never forget. I asked her what she was doing out here, and she told me she didn't have anywhere to live so she had to get some money to rent a hotel room for the night. I looked at her and asked if she would come with me. I assured her we could figure out how to supply her needs of food and a room for the night, but I wanted to talk with her about something more important if she would just be willing to come to my church for a few minutes.

"You don't want me in your church," she said, looking at me suspiciously. "I'm an alcoholic. I've got a bottle of vodka right over there." She pointed to a bag that was lying in the dirt a few feet away. I told her I didn't care about that, if she would just come with me. She grabbed me and hugged me and whispered in my ear, "I'm just not ready." Then she pushed me away and said loudly, "Get out of here. You're messing up my money!" She hugged me again saying, "I know what you're trying to do. I'm just not ready." Then she pushed me away again. She went back and forth like this a number of times.

I knew she may have been drunk at the time or dealing with some type of mental disorder, but I also believe I saw something else happening in those moments. I had a front row seat to the war of good versus evil that was raging within her. I saw something that surprised me when I looked into Lorraine's eyes. I expected to see nothing but death there, but instead I believe God allowed me to see a little of what He sees when He looks at Lorraine. I saw a beautiful woman created in the image of God. I saw hope. I saw a little glimmer of life.

After a lengthy conversation, I couldn't get Lorraine to come with me. I can't tell you how heartbroken I was, but I also know a person has to be ready and I had no control over that. My encounter with Lorraine made a huge impact on me. We drove back to the church, and I was very emotional because of what I had just experienced. I was in the choir loft in the middle of the service, weeping as I thought back on what had just happened, and I believe God spoke to my heart. I looked out at the congregation, and God began to show me that I need to do more to help the "Lorraines" of this world—those that feel hopeless and need their basic physical needs met. He reminded me of Matthew 25:34-36 that says, *"Then the King will say to those on his right, 'Come you who are blessed by my Father; take your inheritance, the kingdom prepared for you since the creation of the world. For I was hungry and*

*you gave me something to eat, I was thirsty and you gave
me something to drink, I was a stranger and you invited me
in, I needed clothes and you clothed me, I was sick and you
looked after me, I was in prison and you came to visit me.'"*

Don't Settle for Crumbs

We definitely have a responsibility to help those around
us. God, also, has shown me that our world today is filled
with *spiritually* starved Lorraines. How many are scouring
in the dirt—and, yes, even in the church pews—looking for
whatever crumbs drop from God's table, when God
Himself has extended an invitation to them to sit at His
table and dine with Him? How many times have I, myself,
settled for crumbs? He has so much to offer us, but most of
us have become so accustomed to the crumbs that we don't
even know the difference between crumbs and a full meal
anymore! The God of the universe calls us to sit at His table
and dine with Him, yet many of us are content to still scour
the dirt, looking for whatever morsels we can find. People
are starving to death spiritually, and they don't even know
it. They're looking to fill their spiritual stomachs with
whatever will temporarily make the hunger go away. Many
get their bellies filled up on Sunday morning but go into
starvation mode on Monday morning until the following
Sunday. They hear a measure of truth but don't apply it or
pursue the presence of God the rest of the week.

Called to Be the Light

We are to be the light that shines on the table of God and illuminates all that He has for His children to eat. We are to show the rest of the world where they can find food and never hunger again and where they can find water and never thirst again. God can only empower us to accomplish this if we are willing vessels walking in His truth. Psalm 139:16 says, *"All the days ordained for me were written in your book before one of them came to be."* And Ephesians 2:10 states it quite clearly, *"For we are God's workmanship, created in Christ Jesus to do good works, which God prepared in advance for us to do."* Make no mistake—you are one-of-a-kind with a unique calling.

What a privilege it is to pour our lives out on behalf of God and His Kingdom. It's not only a privilege, but it is also a necessity. It's in our human nature to be self-focused or self-absorbed, which always leads to an unhealthy outlook on life. If we're not careful, everything quickly becomes about us—our feelings and wants. The next thing we know, we become consumed with our own problems and issues and begin to wallow in worry and regret, which eventually leads to depression.

Shortly after my Lorraine encounter, I found myself in this vicious cycle of self-absorption and depression. I decided the only way to break the cycle was to start playing a more tangible role in helping others. I contacted a local organization that dealt with women who were victims of domestic violence and volunteered a few hours of my time. Since then I have become involved with another organization as well. It's good to be reminded of the needs that are out there and to be involved in helping to meet those needs. Those experiences helped me to walk out of my own pity party and to get my eyes off of myself and back to the reality of the needs of others.

A passage from Isaiah 58 has become a theme for my life and ministry, specifically verses 6-9 which say, *"Is not this the kind of fasting I have chosen to loose the chains of injustice and untie the cords of the yoke, to set the oppressed free and break every yoke? Is it not to share your food with the hungry and to provide the poor wanderer with shelter—when you see the naked, to clothe him, and not to turn away from your own flesh and blood? Then your light will break forth like the dawn and your healing will quickly appear; then your righteousness will go before you, and the glory of the Lord will be your rear guard. Then you will call, and the Lord will answer; you will cry for help, and he will say: Here am I."* Verses 11-12 go on to say, *"The Lord will guide you always; he will satisfy your needs in a sun-scorched land and will strengthen your frame. You will be like a well-watered garden, like a spring whose waters never fail. Your people will rebuild the ancient ruins and will raise up the age-old foundations; you will be called Repairer of Broken Walls, Restorer of Streets with Dwellings."*

Repaired to Be a Restorer

I first became aware of this passage when I received an email from a minister in Africa. She told me she was specifically praying verse 12 over Brian and me and our ministry. When I took out my Bible and read that verse and the ones that preceded it, I became overwhelmed with emotion as I reflected on how God was in the process of repairing my own broken walls and restoring the streets where I travel on this journey known as my life. He is indeed the ultimate Repairer and Restorer and because His Holy Spirit lives within me I can in turn go out and repair and restore in His Name.

God makes a powerful promise to us in these verses. He says in essence if we care for others and pour our lives out for them on His behalf, then our light will break forth and our own healing will quickly appear. Could it be that there is a connection between what we do for others and our own healing? This Scripture makes it clear that is the case.

We are to help others because there are great needs in this world, and our involvement may be the only light that shines in the darkness of a particular situation. A friend shared recently that while on a prayer-walking journey in southern Spain, she and her husband were praying as they walked on a sidewalk that had many lines drawn in the concrete. Spain is often called a missionary's graveyard because it is very difficult to impact this secular society. As they were walking along, the Lord spoke to her and said,

"You may be the *only* person who has ever prayed for the people you are passing on this street." That was a heart-wrenching reality. So, as she stepped on each line in the concrete, she prayed for a person on the street or in the city to be represented by each line. She said it put an all new meaning to each prayer as they walked. We may never know how a prayer for a stranger will be answered.

We have been blessed beyond measure, and it's only right that we give something back, whether it's our time, talents, or resources. But God knows something else about us that most of us don't realize. There are great needs in others, but many times the greatest need is found within our own souls. Sometimes by reaching out we're the ones who are ultimately helped more than those we reach out to.

MANY TIMES THE GREATEST NEED IS FOUND WITHIN OUR OWN SOULS.

Blindsided by the Enemy

God has a plan and a purpose for each one of us, and even those of us who are walking with the Lord can be blindsided by the enemy when we least expect it. Missy's story shared below is just such an example of a young wife and mother innocently becoming entangled with an addiction to prescription drugs. It took a dear friend's tough love to help break Missy free and allow her to see the purpose in her pain.

My life seemed to be similar to a lot of others, pretty normal. It took a while for me to see it that way, because Satan wants us to believe that the pain in our lives sets us apart, makes us different, even unloveable.

I'm a daughter. A wife. A mom. A follower of Christ. I am also an addict.

I was raised in church by parents who love me, and at a young age, I came to a saving knowledge of Jesus Christ. Most things in life came easily to me and difficulties were rare. I'm grateful to have attended a wonderful Christian university, along with my future husband, Jay.

A short while after we married, we moved to the Carolinas where Jay began a new job. If there was ever a person who resisted change, it was me. Suddenly, it seemed that nearly everything changed at once!

In a period of four-and-a-half years, God blessed us with three beautiful children. Life was exactly what I had planned, but I was constantly frustrated by exhaustion and felt overwhelmed. With Jay so busy, I convinced myself that I must care for my family and home on my own. I didn't allow anyone to see my need, much less help. I pushed everyone away, including my husband. I prayed superficial prayers, but I wasn't aware of the depth of my need for a love-relationship with the Lord.

The demands of motherhood, running a household, helping Jay with a new business, and a classic case of postpartum depression began to take their toll. Things were falling apart inside, but appearances were key. What if someone saw me for what I really was? I was so lonely and the void inside grew bigger everyday, but I determind that no one, including the Lord, would be able to love me if my deepest secrets were discovered. And so through smiles, busyness, and lies—the charade continued.

Satan knew my weaknesses and began to take full advantage. After the birth of our youngest son, I realized the pain medication I had been given was helpful in more than one way. At first it relieved the physical discomfort that followed my C-Section, but a gradual shift took place in my thinking as I began to realize that after taking the medication, if only for a short while, things seemed a little better. The comfort found in one valid prescription was short-lived, and I began to devise all sorts of schemes to get more scripts. As time went by the drug became my escape. More and more it was the only thing that took the edge off and filled the emptiness inside.

I bought into the deceiver's lies: "You're not hurting anyone." "You deserve this." "You're not doing anything wrong." "It is a prescription after all." "You can stop anytime you want to."

The truth was I had become a full-blown addict. The drug had somehow become the single most important thing to me. It was the idol I worshipped, as I placed it before my Lord Jesus, my husband, my children, and anything else that mattered.

God tried many different ways to open my eyes to the destruction I was creating, but I ignored all of His gentle discipline. So in His infinite mercy and wisdom, God allowed me to hit rock bottom. I was arrested for prescription fraud, and suddenly, I stood to lose everything, even my husband and children. The lies of addiction had taken their toll on my health, my spiritual condition, and my family. I was completely humiliated, and I couldn't see how my life could ever be restored. In the ugliest, most unimaginable way, I had fallen into the pit of darkness, the pit of pain, terror, and despair. Absolutely nothing in my own strength or wisdom could save me. I was totaly helpless.

His help came in a way that had I not been so desperate I would not have accepted. Through the insistance of a loving friend, Jay and I met with a Christian counselor who specialized in addictions.

As we talked, I noticed her credentials on the wall, and my eyes were drawn to one particular diploma. She had graduated from the same Christian university in Indiana that Jay and I had attended. Instantly, I knew that God was in the midst of my circumstances, and I was finally ready to surrender myself to Him—ALL of myself.

His plan of deliverance took me to a 28-day, inpatient treatment facility an hour away from home. Leaving my husband, my children, and my home was one of the most difficult things I've ever had to do.

A crushing fear paralyzed me the very first morning of treatment, and all I could do was pray. I had finally come to the end of myself. Jesus was there all along, but I couldn't see Him until I reached the point of total surrender and admitted that apart from Him there was nothing that could help me. In that very moment, Jesus Himself took my hand and pulled me out of the pit. His amazing love washed over me in even the secret places that no one had ever seen before. Shame and fear were replaced by peace, forgiveness, and joy in His presence. He is restoring me still day by day. My sin is forgiven because the blood of Jesus covers it all. He is repairing my damaged relationships, especially with my husband and family, and giving us something much more beautiful than we ever had before.

There are still consequences of my actions that I must face, but as these trials come God comforts me with His words to Paul in 2 Corinthians 12:9, "*My grace is sufficient for you, for my power is made perfect in weakness.*" He allowed me to go so far in my sin that my eyes were opened to how truly weak I am without Him.

I praise Him for in my weakness He is strong. I praise Him because He alone is worthy. He alone is sufficient. He is truly all I need.

⁂

God empowered Missy to face her addiction. She found the strength to walk out her freedom once she surrendered to His loving care. If you are ensnared by the enemy's lies or deception in any area of your life, don't be afraid to face up to it and seek help. Missy couldn't do it alone and neither can you. Surrender it to God and seek help from loved ones and Christian counselors who are available to assist you.

Many of us are still searching for our own spiritual and emotional healing. At times God calls us to step out of our comfort zones, to walk away from our pride and self-absorption, and get help. Sometimes getting help and healing comes in the form of serving others. What a miraculous process this is! Physical needs can be met and that ultimately opens a doorway for spiritual needs to be met both in others as well as ourselves. It's awe-inspiring to see this truth lived out each day as we give our lives away.

God's hand is always outstretched to us. All He asks is for us to take His hand and reach out to serve others on His behalf. He can empower us to be changed and to literally change the world. Believe it! He has an amazing work for each of us to do!

⁂

Freedom Fact: *"I can do everything through Him who gives me strength,"* (Philippians 4:13).

What keeps you settling for crumbs when God has a full meal for you to eat?

Do you sense God calling you to get involved in feeding both the physically and spiritually hungry? What is one thing you will do this week to help one person? What are your plans for next week and the week after? (Be specific in setting some realistic goals.)

Freedom Prayer:

Dear Heavenly Father,

I want to be empowered to make a difference in this world on behalf of You and Your Kingdom. Give me the courage to get involved where I see You at work even if that means taking a step out of my comfort zone and trying something new. There are so many physically and spiritually starving people in the world that the task can seem daunting. Break my heart in this area, so I never become calloused to the deep needs that are around me. I want to be a light that shines in this dark world. I want to touch as many as I can on Your behalf taking it one day at a time. Lead me to the specific area that You want me to serve, so I can be in the center of Your will. By the power of Your Holy Spirit use me to repair and restore others in Your Name. I will be faithful to continually point others to You, the Great Lover of our souls.

I praise You for the way You will transform my life in return for serving others. As Your Scripture says, You will surely satisfy my needs and make me a well-watered garden. Use me to make a difference for Your glory!

Amen.

CHAPTER 5

Our Choice

CHOOSING FREEDOM EACH DAY

*"You did not choose me, but I chose you
and appointed you to go and bear fruit—
fruit that will last."*

JOHN 15:16A

Living in freedom is a choice. I know I can't control certain things in life. However, it's what I do when those things occur and to whom I turn for guidance and direction that makes all the difference in how my life unfolds.

God created us with the power of choice, but be aware that we have an enemy who wants us to think we have no choice, as he whispers, "Things are what they are, and you are powerless." Each morning he will taunt us with lies and

GOD CREATED
US WITH THE
POWER OF
CHOICE.

words of discouragement. Will we listen to his words or will we choose to walk in the truth of God's Word? I have to admit there are days when I choose poorly, but more often than not, I choose wisely because I have learned to trust in the promises of a loving God who knows what is best for me.

Pruned by Love

Chapter 15 in the book of John reminds us that Christ is the true Vine and we are the branches. We must remain in Him in order to bear fruit. This requires a pruning process to take place in our lives that can be painful and uncomfortable. But when our Father prunes us, He always does it out of love and with the greatest of care. If you remain in Him, He will remain in you. It's one of His most precious promises that you can count on no matter what you may face.

It is definitely easier to just "talk the talk," but it's in "walking the walk" that our lives are truly transformed for the Kingdom of God—realizing that we have a choice to make no matter what comes our way. It's in learning to trust God even in the most painful, uncertain moments of life that we can truly be set free. He is the One who loves us more than life itself, and He is the One who tells us each and every day that we are worthy in His sight. We may never hear those words from our spouses, friends, children, or co-workers, but we hear it every day from God if we choose to hear it. He proved our worth to Him when He sent His Son to die on a cross for us. What a personal act of love that was. With that sacrificial act, we were all given the opportunity to be made new, and that fact completely overwhelms me.

The Importance of Trust

I truly believe in being open and honest with God. There have been times in my life when I have felt utter despair and haven't had any idea what was happening. In those moments of consuming emotion, I've only seen two options for handling the situation: turn my back on God or press into Him. Sometimes pressing in means we must wrestle with Him. That's right. If you are in the middle of a deep valley in your life and you want to turn away from Him, I say stay in the fight and wrestle with Him. If you're tempted to walk away out of anger or pain, I say wrestle instead every time! Tell God exactly what you're feeling— no matter how bad it may be. He already knows what's going on inside of you, so you may as well just confess it and get it all out on the table. If you're angry, tell Him. If you're bitter, tell Him. If you're confused and not sure how to trust Him, tell Him. Ask Him the tough questions. At least when you're wrestling, you're still in it with Him and focusing on Him! I'm a wrestler for better or worse, and

God in His great mercy has allowed me to wrestle with Him until I find the victory He has purposed for me.

Psalm 13 is one of my favorite wrestling Psalms. It says, *"How long, O Lord? Will you forget me forever? How long will you hide your face from me? How long must I wrestle with my thoughts and every day have sorrow in my heart? How long will my enemy triumph over me? Look on me and answer, O Lord my God. Give light to my eyes, or I will sleep in death; my enemy will say, 'I have overcome him,' and my foes will rejoice when I fall."*

If that isn't David wrestling with God, then I don't know what is. I know many people would never dream of wrestling, but I say as long as it's honest and true to where you're at, do it. There's no sense in hiding or trying to be less than honest with Him, because He is all-knowing.

God doesn't always answer our questions in the way or manner in which we may want. There are certain things we will never have answers to this side of heaven and things we will never truly understand with our finite minds, so in the end we must simply trust Him. After the time of purging is done and after we've come to the end of our strength, whether we have the answers we want or not, we MUST trust.

At the end of Psalm 13 after David has wrestled and cried out to God he says this, *"But I trust in your unfailing love; my heart rejoices in your salvation. I will sing to the Lord, for he has been good to me."* No matter what circumstances I am in, I know that I can trust in His unfailing love.

Proverbs 3:5-6 sums it up quite nicely, *"Trust in the Lord with all your heart and lean not on your own understanding; in all your ways acknowledge him, and he will make your paths straight."*

Trust His Heart

Babbie Mason wrote an amazing song about trusting God called, *"Trust His Heart."* I recorded it a few years ago. The lyric of the chorus says, "God is too wise to be mistaken / God is too good to be unkind / So when you don't understand / When you don't see His plan / When you can't trace His hand / Trust His heart."

> GOD IS TOO WISE TO BE MISTAKEN.

God has our best at His heart, and we must choose to believe that.

As Kristin shares her story below, you'll see how God healed her soul in the midst of a heart-breaking tragedy and became her "everything." As she leaned on Him and learned how to totally trust Him in the face of dire circumstances, He gave her peace in the midst of the storm and restored her life abundantly. I chose the song, *"Trust His Heart,"* to accompany her story on our *Finally Free* CD because it so perfectly spoke to what she had experienced.

The first time I met Andy we were in the same business class in college, and he was a familiar face from the fraternity house next door. I didn't realize that meeting Andy would change my life forever, but God did.

Our courtship began in college; and after dating for several years, we married. We were a pretty "normal" couple with highs and lows, and I was crazy in love with him. In fact, I thought my husband was "my everything." God knew better.

My parents divorced when I was young. Growing up it was Mom, my sister, and me. I never really understood why Dad left. Consequently, I spent a lot of time looking for love and reassurance from all the wrong people. I started following Jesus in high school, but didn't really begin to understand what that meant until I met Andy's mom, Connie. This woman lived out, every day, what it meant to be a person of conviction and to live a life based on prayer. Connie encouraged both of us to get "grounded" in our spiritual life. What a blessing she has always been to me.

Our story seemed to follow a pretty common path until one spring day. I came home from work to find Andy immersed in the bathtub trying to get a very high fever to come down. After a couple of days, he was hospitalized and put through a whole battery of tests. Whatever was wrong with Andy remained a mystery. That summer, Andy became moody and quiet. His mom and I thought he was depressed. Andy was a scratch golfer, but that summer, he started pulling his shots to the left. In my immaturity, I just prayed for whatever was bothering Andy to go away.

At the end of the summer, I received a call from Andy's work that changed everything. Andy had stood up to give a presentation, and, in that moment, he forgot who he was and why he was there. We rushed to him and immediately admitted him to the hospital. After several CAT scans and an MRI, we learned that Andy's brain was under attack from a massive viral infection. All that summer it had been infecting his brain. The disease was very rare and the prognosis was not good. At that time, we had been married only one year.

Waiting in the surgery area, I remember praying that God would make it all right. I begged Him not to take "my everything" from me. I had already been through that when my Dad left. I had so many questions, too many to recite.

When the surgeon came out to talk to us, I knew something was seriously wrong. He said he was very sorry, but there was nothing they could do. Andy might have six more months with us.

Andy's mom moved in with us to help take care of him while I was at work. In the fall, he began to have seizures and could not be left alone. His mind began to deteriorate. He was bound to a wheelchair and had to be helped with the most basic of needs.

We had more questions and fewer answers. One thing, however, never changed, God continued to show us His never-ending love.

At Christmas time, Andy and I received the best gift we could have received. God gave Andy clarity of mind for two weeks. We spent that time saying all the things we wanted to say before it was too late. We laughed and cried and laughed again. We said goodbye.

Two weeks after Christmas, Andy went into a coma and never woke up. His mom and I spent the last 24 hours by his side. Our friends came, our church came, and it was a time of celebrating Andy's life. We knew God was there as well. Andy was 26 when he died and I was a 25-year-old widow.

During the funeral I felt this incredible sense of being carried, and I was stronger than I could have imagined. People commented during the months that followed, that they could not believe how well I was doing. I used that time to share my story. Through my loss, God provided loving arms to carry me. I began to learn that God was truly "my everything."

I don't know a lot, but I am sure of a few things: God will never give us more than we can handle, and He can be trusted in even the most painful circumstances. Andy reached more people for Christ in his death than he had in his life.

A few years after Andy went to be with the Lord, I remarried and now have two beautiful children. God has taken the broken pieces of my life—all my losses and disappointments—and made something beautiful out of them. Only He can do that and I'm forever grateful. He is truly "my everything"!

※◎◎※

I can't stress the issue of trust enough. This has been a really tough one for me through the years, because I'm prone to worry. I have discovered that worry is directly related to disbelief. What a moment that was in my life when I discovered I had an issue with believing God. Not believing IN God, but believing God and His promises are true. There is a difference. A point comes in each of our lives when we have to say through our actions, "Yes, I believe God," or "No, I don't."

God Is Good All the Time

In Romans 8:28 Paul states, *"And we know that in all things God works for the good of those who love him, who have been called according to his purpose."* For many years I read that Scripture skimming over a very important three-letter word—*all*. In ALL things God works for the good of those who love Him. That means He has the power to work in the good things, in the difficult or painful things over which we have no control, and yes, even in our mistakes. He can make all things conform to His ultimate pattern of good for us. He is not confined to our concept of time, and He is certainly not confined to our thoughts or mistakes, regardless of how big or small they may seem. Nothing confines or binds Him. God truly can do the unimaginable and make something magnificent out of the messiest situations in our lives.

> GOD TRULY CAN DO THE UNIMAGINABLE.

If you've found yourself going down the wrong road or if you are consumed with regret over mistakes in your life, stop right now and confess that to God. Ask Him to heal and forgive, and then watch Him work. If your life has been turned upside down by tragedy or difficult circumstances that are out of control, trust Him to carry you through them. Remember—He lives above our circumstances, and He calls us to join Him there, believing He can work *all* things for our good.

Choose God and His freedom, my friend. No matter how difficult it may be or how unreasonable it may seem—Choose God and His freedom!

Be encouraged as you read this powerful letter written from a father to his child from the book, *The Lost Choice* by Andy Andrews.[1]

CHOOSE GOD AND HIS FREEDOM!

I made you different from the others.

On the planet Earth, there has never been one like you...and there never will be again.

Your spirit, your thoughts and feelings, your ability to reason—all exist in no one else.

Your eyes are a masterpiece, incomparable, and windows to a soul that is also uniquely yours.

A single strand of your hair has been created especially for you. Of the multitudes who have come before you and the multitudes who may follow, not one of them duplicates the formula with which I made you. I made you different from the others.

The blood that flows through your veins flows through the heart of one whom I have chosen. The rarities that make you one of a kind, my child, are no mere accident or quirk of fate.

I made you different in order that you might make a difference.

You have been created with the ability to change the world. Every single choice you make...every single action you take...matters. But remember, the converse is also true. Every choice you do not make...every action you do not take...matters just as much!

Your actions cannot be hoarded, saved for later, or used selectively. By your hand, millions of lives will be altered, caught up in a chain of events begun by you this very day. But the opposite is true as well. Millions of lives are also altered, caught up in an entirely different chain of events—if you choose to wait.

You possess the power of choice. Free will. You have been given everything you need to act, but the choice is yours alone. And beginning this very moment, you will choose wisely.

Now go. And never feel inadequate again. Do not dwell in thoughts of insignificance or wander aimlessly lost, like a sheep.

You are powerful. You matter. And you have been found.

You are my choice.

Your Father

God has already made His choice. He chose you. Now what will you choose?

※⊙◈◎※

Freedom Fact: *"You did not choose me, but I chose you and appointed you to go and bear fruit—fruit that will last,"* (John 15:16).

Ask the Lord to reveal any area of your life where you may still be bound or weighed down by a sack of stones.

Are you ready to release your stones? Why or why not?

Throughout the day affirm your trust in God by simply whispering, *"I trust you, Heavenly Father."*

Freedom Prayer:

Dear Heavenly Father,

I realize I have a choice to make. Thank You for loving me enough to give me the power of choice. Today, Father, I choose You and Your freedom. I release the things that have been keeping me bound for years. I am Your child and You never meant for me to live in bondage. You came to set us free so I am claiming Your freedom today! Give me the power to make this same choice each and every day.

I will trust You as I walk this freedom journey hand-in-hand with You. I will keep my eyes fixed on You, because You have the power to restore my life and bring more joy and peace to it than I could ever imagine. I am empowered to bear much fruit for Your glory. Thank You for setting me free in the Mighty Name of Jesus!

Amen.

CONCLUSION

God *IS* Love

God *IS* love and love is, therefore, the foundation of freedom. It's out of love that God gives us each the ability to choose true freedom in Him. To be free to love unhindered is one of God's greatest gifts. It allows us to let go of fear, hurt, rejection, and pain while still loving Him and others with utter abandon, regardless of the cost.

With love as our foundation, we have the freedom to choose between God's way and the world's way. It's the difference between flourishing and just barely surviving. I would much rather dance in His freedom and joy—living my life to the fullest—than to limp through life trying to endure the world's system of bondage and fear.

Keeping our *focus* on God and having the courage to allow Him to lead us through *restoration* into *enjoyment* and ultimately *empowerment* is the journey He desires for all of us.

I leave you with these words from Colossians 2:6-7, "*So then, just as you received Christ Jesus as Lord, continue to live in him, rooted and built up in him, strengthened in the faith as you were taught, and overflowing with thankfulness.*" It is my prayer that you would strive to be rooted in Christ and in turn be strengthened in your faith, which will lead to a deeper understanding of the height, depth and breadth of His love for you. It is only then that your heart will begin to overflow with true thankfulness realizing you are free to live and love as He intended. Yes, you have the power to be free, my precious friends. Now put your hand in His and joyfully walk with Him in the freedom He has ordained for you!

ENDNOTES

Introduction

[1]Max Lucado, *When God Whispers Your Name* (Dallas: Word Publishing, 1994), pp. 117-122.

Chapter 2

[1]John Eldredge, *Waking the Dead* (Nashville: Thomas Nelson Publishers, 2003), p. 141.

Chapter 3

[1]Brennan Manning, *Ruthless Trust* (New York: HarperCollins Publishers, 2000), pp. 133-135, 138,141.

[2]Ibid.

Chapter 5

[1]Andy Andrews, *The Lost Choice* (Nashville: Thomas Nelson Publishers, 2004), pp. 229-230.

A Call to Salvation

If you have turned to this section of the book, you must be interested in finding out more about how to have a relationship with Jesus Christ. The word *relationship* is really the key. There may be a number of reasons you don't have a relationship with Christ right now. Perhaps no one has ever talked with you about it. Maybe you grew up in a church where the people wounded you or someone you love. It's possible the only Christians you know haven't been very good examples of God and His love. Whatever the reason might be, please don't let the failures of human beings keep you from having a relationship with God.

The bottom line is this. There is a God and He is crazy in love with you. He desires a relationship with you and after you leave this life He wants you to be with Him for all of eternity in heaven. Romans 3:23-24 says, *"Since we've*

*compiled this long and sorry record as sinners and proved
that we are utterly incapable of living the glorious lives
God wills for us, God did it for us. Out of sheer generosity
he put us in right standing with himself. A pure gift. He got
us out of the mess we're in and restored us to where he
always wanted us to be. And he did it by means of Jesus
Christ,"* (THE MESSAGE).

We have all sinned, and that separates us from God. But
God did something loving and daring to bring us back into
relationship with Him. He sent His one and only Son, Jesus
Christ, down to earth to die on a cross for our sins. Jesus
took all of our sins upon Himself, and He paid the price for
us. He died on the cross and then rose from the dead three
days later, conquering sin and death and, in turn, making a
way for all of us to spend eternity in heaven with Him. John
3:16 says, *"This is how much God loved the world: He
gave his Son, his one and only Son. And this is why: so that
no one need be destroyed; by believing in him, anyone can
have a whole and lasting life,"* (THE MESSAGE).

Salvation is a free gift. There is no way to earn your way
to heaven. None of us can ever be good enough. Christ
already did everything that needed to be done on the cross
more than 2,000 years ago. All we have to do is accept His
free gift. He won't force us to accept it. God doesn't want
an army of robots following Him. He wants people legitimately in love with Him in the same way He loves them.
God's promise to us is stated this way: *"Look at me. I stand*

at the door. I knock. If you hear me call and open the door,
I'll come right in," (Revelation 3:20 THE MESSAGE).

If you are ready to accept Jesus Christ as your Lord and
Savior, please say this prayer right now:

Dear Heavenly Father,

I believe I'm a sinner, but I also believe You sent
Your Son, Jesus Christ, to die on a cross for my sins
and that after three days He rose from the dead
conquering sin and death. Please forgive me of my
sin and come into my heart to be the Lord of my life.
Change me and make me into the person You want
me to be. I thank You that You not only see me as I
am today, but You see all that I can be through You!
I love You, Father, and I thank You for saving me!

Amen.

Now I want to encourage you to do one more thing. It
is very important to find a church to attend—some place
you feel comfortable and can begin to study the Bible and
grow in your faith. Spend time with other Christians that
can encourage you and lift you up. Begin to get to know the
God who has such deep love and affection for you by setting
aside time to be with Him on a regular basis. Studying the
Bible will be a vital part of your journey as well.

As you begin to get involved in a church family, talk
with the pastor about being baptized. This is another

important step. The Bible teaches that we should make our profession of faith through baptism. In Mark 16:16, Jesus said, *"Whoever believes and is baptized will be saved, but whoever does not believe will be condemned."* Baptism symbolizes our own spiritual death and resurrection. It's a celebration and profession of our faith in Jesus Christ.

Welcome to the family of God! I am thrilled to have a new friend in Christ, and I'm so thankful for you!

Freedom Facts for Specific Issues

Abandonment/Rejection

Zephaniah 3:17—*The Lord your God is with you, he is mighty to save. He will take great delight in you, he will quiet you with his love, he will rejoice over you with singing.*

Psalm 145:18-19—*The Lord is near to all who call on him, to all who call on him in truth. He fulfills the desires of those who fear him; he hears their cry and saves them.*

Addiction

2 Corinthians 5:17—*Therefore if anyone is in Christ, he is a new creation; the old has gone, the new has come!*

2 Corinthians 10:5—*We demolish arguments and every pretension that sets itself up against the knowledge of God, and we take captive every thought to make it obedient to Christ.*

Anger

Psalm 37:8—*Refrain from anger and turn from wrath; do not fret—it leads only to evil.*

Ephesians 4:26-27—*In your anger do not sin. Do not let the sun go down while you are still angry, and do not give the devil a foothold.*

James 1:19-20—*My dear brothers, take note of this: Everyone should be quick to listen, slow to speak and slow to become angry, for man's anger does not bring about the righteous life that God desires.*

Anxiety/Stress

Philippians 4:6-7—*Do not be anxious about anything, but in everything, by prayer and petition, with thanksgiving, present your requests to God. And the peace of God, which transcends all understanding, will guard your hearts and your minds in Christ Jesus.*

Philippians 4:19—*And my God will meet all your needs according to his glorious riches in Christ Jesus.*

1 Peter 5:7—*Cast all your anxiety on him because he cares for you.*

Psalm 94:19—*When anxiety was great within me, your consolation brought joy to my soul.*

Bitterness

Ephesians 4:31-32—*Get rid of all bitterness, rage and anger, brawling and slander, along with every form of malice. Be kind and compassionate to one another, forgiving each other, just as in Christ God forgave you.*

Hebrews 12:15—*See to it that no one misses the grace of God and that no bitter root grows up to cause trouble and defile many.*

Defeating Negativity

Ephesians 4:29—*Do not let any unwholesome talk come out of your mouths, but only what is helpful for building others up according to their needs, that it may benefit those who listen.*

Philippians 2:14-15—*Do everything without complaining or arguing, so that you may become blameless and pure, children of God without fault in a crooked and depraved generation in which you shine like stars in the universe.*

Philippians 4:8—*Finally, brothers, whatever is true, whatever is noble, whatever is right, whatever is pure, whatever is lovely, whatever is admirable—if anything is excellent or praiseworthy— think about such things.*

Depression

Psalm 13:1-2, 5-6—*How long, O Lord? Will you forget me forever? How long will you hide your face from me? How long must I wrestle with my thoughts and every day have sorrow in my heart? How long will my enemy triumph over me?... But I trust in your unfailing love; my heart rejoices in your salvation. I will sing to the Lord for he has been good to me.*

Psalm 42:11—*Why are you downcast, O my soul? Why so disturbed within me? Put your hope in God, for I will yet praise him, my Savior and my God.*

Psalm 119:76—*May your unfailing love be my comfort, according to your promise to your servant.*

Failure

Psalm 121:1-2—*I lift up my eyes to the hills—where does my help come from? My help comes from the Lord, the Maker of heaven and earth.*

117

Psalm 145:14—*The Lord upholds all those who fall and lifts up all who are bowed down.*

Isaiah 43:18—*Forget the former things; do not dwell on the past. See, I am doing a new thing! Now it springs up; do you not perceive it?*

Philippians 3:13-14—*Brothers, I do not consider myself yet to have taken hold of it. But one thing I do: Forgetting what is behind and straining toward what is ahead, I press on toward the goal to win the prize for which God has called me heavenward in Christ Jesus.*

Faith

Psalm 145:13b—*The Lord is faithful to all his promises and loving toward all he has made.*

2 Corinthians 4:18—*So we fix our eyes not on what is seen, but on what is unseen. For what is seen is temporary, but what is unseen is eternal.*

Galatians 6:9—*Let us not become weary in doing good, for at the proper time we will reap a harvest if we do not give up.*

Hebrews 11:1—*Now faith is being sure of what we hope for and certain of what we do not see.*

Fear

Joshua 1:9—*Have I not commanded you? Be strong and courageous. Do not be terrified; do not be discouraged, for the Lord your God will be with you wherever you go.*

Psalm 23:4—*Even though I walk through the valley of the shadow of death, I will fear no evil for you are with me; your rod and your staff they comfort me.*

Psalm 27:1—*The Lord is my light and my salvation—whom shall I fear? The Lord is the stronghold of my life—of whom shall I be afraid?*

Psalm 46:1-2—*God is our refuge and strength, an ever-present help in trouble. Therefore we will not fear, though the earth give way and the mountains fall into the heart of the sea, though its waters roar and foam and the mountains quake with their surging.*

Isaiah 41:10—*So do not fear, for I am with you; do not be dismayed, for I am your God. I will strengthen you and help you; I will uphold you with my righteous right hand.*

Isaiah 41:13—*For I am the Lord, your God, who takes hold of your right hand and says to you, Do not fear; I will help you.*

Isaiah 43:1-3a—*Fear not, for I have redeemed you; I have summoned you by name; you are mine. When you pass through the waters, I will be with you; and when you pass through the rivers, they will not sweep over you. When you walk through the fire, you will not be burned; the flames will not set you ablaze. For I am the Lord, your God, the Holy One of Israel, your Savior.*

John 14:27—*Peace I leave with you; my peace I give you. I do not give to you as the world gives. Do not let your hearts be troubled and do not be afraid.*

Hebrews 13:6—*So we say with confidence, "The Lord is my helper; I will not be afraid. What can man do to me?"*

Freedom from Bondage

Psalm 118:5—*In my anguish I cried to the Lord, and he answered by setting me free.*

John 8:36—*So if the Son sets you free, you will be free indeed.*

Galatians 5:1—*It is for freedom that Christ has set us free. Stand firm then, and do not let yourselves be burdened again by a yoke of slavery.*

Grief

Isaiah 61:1-3—*The Spirit of the Sovereign Lord is on me, because the Lord has anointed me to preach good news to the poor. He has sent me to bind up the brokenhearted, to proclaim freedom for the captives and release from darkness for the prisoners, to proclaim the year of the Lord's favor and the day of vengeance of our God, to comfort all who mourn, and provide for those who grieve in Zion—to bestow on them a crown of beauty instead of ashes, the oil of gladness instead of mourning, and a garment of praise instead of a spirit of despair. They will be called oaks of righteousness, a planting of the Lord for the display of his splendor.*

Isaiah 53:3a—*He was despised and rejected by men, a man of sorrows, and familiar with suffering.*

Jeremiah 31:13—*Then maidens will dance and be glad, young men and old as well. I will turn their mourning into gladness; I will give them comfort and joy instead of sorrow.*

2 Corinthians 1:3-4—*Praise be to the God and Father of our Lord Jesus Christ, the Father of compassion and the God of all comfort, who comforts us in all our troubles, so that we can comfort those in any trouble with the comfort we ourselves have received from God.*

Guilt/Shame

Psalm 25:1-3—*To you, O lord, I lift up my soul; in you I trust, O my God. Do not let me be put to shame, nor let my enemies triumph over me. No one whose hope is in you will ever be put to shame, but they will be put to shame who are treacherous without excuse.*

Psalm 25:20—*Guard my life and rescue me; let me not be put to shame, for I take refuge in you.*

Romans 8:1-2—*Therefore, there is now no condemnation for those who are in Christ Jesus, because through Christ Jesus the law of the Spirit of life set me free from the law of sin and death.*

Romans 10:11—*As the Scripture says, "Anyone who trusts in him will never be put to shame."*

1 Peter 3:18a—*For Christ died for sins once for all, the righteous for the unrighteous, to bring you to God.*

1 John 1:9—*If we confess our sins, he is faithful and just and will forgive us our sins and purify us from all unrighteousness.*

Hope

Psalm 25:4-5—*Show me your ways, O Lord, teach me your paths; guide me in your truth and teach me, for you are God my Savior, and my hope is in you all day long.*

Psalm 31:24—*Be strong and take heart, all you who hope in the Lord.*

Psalm 33:18—*But the eyes of the Lord are on those who fear him, on those whose hope is in his unfailing love.*

Psalm 62:5—*Find rest, O my soul, in God alone; my hope comes from him. He alone is my rock and my salvation; he is my fortress, I will not be shaken.*

Isaiah 40:30-31—*Even youths grow tired and weary, and young men stumble and fall; but those who hope in the Lord will renew their strength. They will soar on wings like eagles; they will run and not grow weary, they will walk and not be faint.*

Lamentations 3:21-26—*Yet this I call to mind and therefore I have hope: Because of the Lord's great love we are not consumed, for his compassions never fail. They are new every morning; great is your faithfulness. I say to myself, "The Lord is my portion; therefore I will wait for him." The Lord is good to those whose hope is in him, to the one who seeks him, it is good to wait quietly for the salvation of the Lord.*

Luke 1:37—*For nothing is impossible with God.*

Romans 5:3-5—*Not only so, but we also rejoice in our sufferings, because we know that suffering produces perseverance; perseverance, character; and character, hope. And hope does not disappoint us, because God has poured out his love into our hearts by the Holy Spirit, whom he has given us.*

Romans 15:4—*For everything that was written in the past was written to teach us, so that through endurance and the encouragement of the Scriptures we might have hope.*

Joy

Psalm 16:11—*You have made known to me the path of life; you will fill me with joy in your presence, with eternal pleasures at your right hand.*

Psalm 28:7—*The Lord is my strength and my shield; my heart trusts in him, and I am helped. My heart leaps for joy and I will give thanks to him in song.*

Psalm 37:4—*Delight yourself in the Lord and he will give you the desires of your heart.*

Psalm 86:4—*Bring joy to your servant, for to you, O Lord, I lift up my soul.*

Psalm 90:14—*Satisfy us in the morning with your unfailing love, that we may sing for joy and be glad all our days.*

John 15:11-12—*I have told you this so that my joy may be in you and that your joy may be complete. My command is this: Love each other as I have loved you.*

1 Thesselonians 5:16-18—*Be joyful always; pray continually; give thanks in all circumstances, for this is God's will for you in Christ Jesus.*

Peace of Mind

Proverbs 9:10—*The fear of the Lord is the beginning of wisdom, and knowledge of the Holy One is understanding.*

Jeremiah 33:3—*Call to me and I will answer you and tell you great and unsearchable things you do not know.*

Romans 12:2—*Do not conform any longer to the pattern of this world, but be transformed by the renewing of your mind. Then you will be able to test and approve what God's will is—his good, pleasing and perfect will.*

Pride

Proverbs 11:2—*When pride comes, then comes disgrace, but with humility comes wisdom.*

Proverbs 13:10—*Pride only breeds quarrels, but wisdom is found in those who take advice.*

Proverbs 29:23—*A man's pride brings him low, but a man of lowly spirit gains honor.*

Galatians 6:3-4—*If anyone thinks he is something when he is nothing, he deceives himself. Each one should test his own actions. Then he can take pride in himself, without comparing himself to somebody else, for each one should carry his own load.*

Strength

Psalm 55:22—*Cast your cares on the Lord and he will sustain you, he will never let the righteous fall.*

Philippians 4:13—*I can do everything through him who gives me strength.*

James 1:12—*Blessed is the man who perseveres under trial, because when he has stood the test, he will receive the crown of life that God has promised to those who love him.*

<u>Trust</u>

Psalm 9:10—*Those who know your name will trust in you, for you, Lord, have never forsaken those who seek you.*

Psalm 13:5—*But I trust in your unfailing love; my heart rejoices in your salvation.*

Psalm 62:8—*Trust in him at all times, O people; pour out your hearts to him, for God is our refuge.*

Psalm 143:8—*Let the morning bring me word of your unfailing love, for I have put my trust in you. Show me the way I should go, for to you I lift up my soul.*

Proverbs 3:5-6—*Trust in the Lord with all your heart and lean not on your own understanding; in all your ways acknowledge him, and he will make your paths straight.*

Isaiah 12:2—*"Surely God is my salvation; I will trust and not be afraid. The Lord, the Lord, is my strength and my song; he has become my salvation."*

Isaiah 26:4—*Trust in the Lord forever, for the Lord, the Lord, is the Rock eternal.*

Isaiah 55:8-9—*"For my thoughts are not your thoughts, neither are your ways my ways," declares the Lord. "As the heavens are higher than the earth, so are my ways higher than your ways and my thoughts than your thoughts."*

John 14:1—*"Do not let your hearts be troubled. Trust in God, trust also in me."*

Worry

Luke 12:22-26—*Then Jesus said to his disciples: "Therefore I tell you, do not worry about your life, what you will eat; or about your body, what you will wear. Life is more than food, and the body more than clothes. Consider the ravens: They do not sow or reap, they have no storeroom or barn; yet God feeds them. And how much more valuable you are than birds! Who of you by worrying can add a single hour to his life? Since you cannot do this very little thing, why do you worry about the rest?*

Romans 8:28—*And we know that in all things God works for the good of those who love him, who have been called according to his purpose.*

Worthiness

Jeremiah 29:11-13—*"For I know the plans I have for you," declares the Lord, "plans to prosper you and not to harm you, plans to give you hope and a future. Then you will call upon me and come and pray to me, and I will listen to you. You will seek me and find me when you seek me with all your heart."*

Zechariah 2:8b—*"For whoever touches you touches the apple of his eye."*

John 15:16a—*You did not choose me, but I chose you and appointed you to go and bear fruit—fruit that will last.*

Romans 5:8—*But God demonstrates his own love for us in this: While we were still sinners, Christ died for us.*

ABOUT THE AUTHOR

Kim Tabor is an artist, worship leader, and author with a deep love for the Lord and a lifelong commitment to serving His Church. For the last 15 years, Kim has been traveling throughout the country sharing her gifts at churches, conferences, and leadership gatherings. Kim combines her amazing vocal gift with the ability to lead people through an experience of worship. Whether sharing in concert or a worship service as an anointed vocalist and worship leader, or speaking at a retreat or women's conference, you will be encouraged and challenged by Kim's ministry. Kim has had the honor of traveling with Sandi Patty and Bill Gaither as well as ministering in some of the most prominent churches in America with her husband, Brian. To find out more about Kim's ministry and how to obtain a copy of the *Finally Free* CD, log on to: www.taborministries.org

Finally Free: Stories Of Hope and Inspiration is a very unique labor of love as seven women share their personal stories combined with Scripture and songs to create a powerful devotional for today's woman. Their stories of healing, restoration, forgiveness, and redemption come together and touch many of the issues women face in their daily walks. It will impact your life and your relationship with the Lord in powerful ways as it challenges you to let go of the past and choose a life of true freedom in Christ.